science for a changing world

Prepared in cooperation with the U.S. Army Corps of Engineers and
the Oregon Department of State Lands

Preliminary Assessment of Channel Stability and Bed-Material Transport along Hunter Creek, Southwestern Oregon

By Krista L. Jones, J. Rose Wallick, Jim E. O'Connor, Mackenzie K. Keith, Joseph F. Mangano, and John C. Risley

Open-File Report 2011–1160

U.S. Department of the Interior
U.S. Geological Survey

U.S. Department of the Interior
KEN SALAZAR, Secretary

U.S. Geological Survey
Marcia K. McNutt, Director

U.S. Geological Survey, Reston, Virginia 2011

For product and ordering information:
World Wide Web: *http://www.usgs.gov/pubprod*
Telephone: 1-888-ASK-USGS

For more information on the USGS—the Federal source for science about the Earth,
its natural and living resources, natural hazards, and the environment:
World Wide Web: *http://www.usgs.gov*
Telephone: 1-888-ASK-USGS Suggested citation:

Jones, K.L, Wallick, J.R., O'Connor, J.E., Keith, M.K., Mangano, J.F., and Risley, J.C., 2011, Preliminary assessment of channel stability and bed-material transport along Hunter Creek, southwestern Oregon: U.S. Geological Survey Open-File Report 2011–1160, 41 p.

Contents

Figures

Tables

Conversion Factors and Datums

Multiply	By	To obtain
Length		
centimeter (cm)	0.3937	inch (in.)
millimeter (mm)	0.03937	inch (in.)
meter (m)	3.281	foot (ft)
kilometer (km)	0.6214	mile (mi)
Area		
square meter (m^2)	10.76	square foot (ft^2)
square kilometer (km^2)	0.3861	square mile (mi^2)
Volume		
cubic meter (m^3)	0.0008107	acre-foot (acre-ft)
cubic meter (m^3)	35.31	cubic foot (ft^3)
cubic meter (m^3)	1.308	cubic yard (yd^3)
Mass		
kilogram (kg)	2.2046	pound avoirdupois (lb)
metric ton (megagram)	1.1023	ton [U.S.]
Flow rate		
cubic meter per second (m^3/s)	35.31	cubic foot per second (ft^3/s)

Vertical coordinate information is referenced to the North American Vertical Datum of 1988 (NAVD 88).

Horizontal coordinate information is referenced to the North American Datum of 1983 (NAD 83).

Elevation, as used in this report, refers to distance above the vertical datum.

Abbreviations, Acronyms, and Symbols

+	positive
<	less than
>	greater than
BLM	Bureau of Land Management
commun.	communication
D_{50}	median diameter
DEM	Digital Elevation Model
DOGAMI	Oregon Department of Geology and Mineral Industries
EA Engineering, Science and Technology	Ecological Analysts Engineering, Science, and Technology
ESRI	Environmental Systems Research Institute, Inc.
GIS	Geographic Information Systems
GLO	General Land Office
LiDAR	Light Detecting and Ranging
NA	not available/applicable
NAD 83	North American Datum of 1983
NAIP	National Agriculture Imagery Program
NAVD 88	North American Vertical Datum of 1988
ODOT	Oregon Department of Transportation
Oregon DOR	Oregon Department of Revenue
PLSS	Public Land Survey System
RI	recurrence interval
RKM	river kilometer
RM	river mile
RMSE	root mean square error
SCS	Soil Conservation Service
UO	University of Oregon
USACE	U.S. Army Corps of Engineers
USFS	U.S. Forest Service
USGS	U.S. Geological Survey
UTM, Zone 10N	Universal Transverse Mercator, Zone 10 North
WAC	Western Aerial Contractor

Preliminary Assessment of Channel Stability and Bed-Material Transport along Hunter Creek, Southwestern Oregon

By Krista L. Jones, J. Rose Wallick, Jim E. O'Connor, Mackenzie K. Keith, Joseph F. Mangano, and John C. Risley

Significant Findings

This preliminary assessment of (1) bed-material transport in the Hunter Creek basin, (2) historical changes in channel condition, and (3) supplementary data needed to inform permitting decisions regarding instream gravel extraction revealed the following:

- Along the lower 12.4 km (kilometers) of Hunter Creek from its confluence with the Little South Fork Hunter Creek to its mouth, the river has confined and unconfined segments and is predominately alluvial in its lowermost 11 km. This 12.4-km stretch of river can be divided into two geomorphically distinct study reaches based primarily on valley physiography. In the Upper Study Reach (river kilometer [RKM] 12.4–6), the active channel comprises a mixed bed of bedrock, boulders, and smaller grains. The stream is confined in the upper 1.4 km of the reach by a bedrock canyon and in the lower 2.4 km by its valley. In the Lower Study Reach (RKM 6–0), where the area of gravel bars historically was largest, the stream flows over bed material that is predominately alluvial sediments. The channel alternates between confined and unconfined segments.

- The primary human activities that likely have affected bed-material transport and the extent and area of gravel bars are (1) historical and ongoing aggregate extraction from gravel bars in the study area and (2) timber harvest and associated road construction throughout the basin. These anthropogenic activities likely have varying effects on sediment transport and deposition throughout the study area and over time. Although assessing the relative effects of these anthropogenic activities on sediment dynamics would be challenging, the Hunter Creek basin may serve as a case study for such an assessment because it is mostly free of other alterations to hydrologic and geomorphic processes such as flow regulation, dredging, and other navigation improvements that are common in many Oregon coastal basins.

- Several datasets are available that may support a more detailed physical assessment of Hunter Creek. The entire study area has been captured in aerial photographs at least once per decade since the 1940s. This temporally rich photograph dataset would support quantitative analyses of changes in channel planform as well as vegetation cover. Light Detection And Ranging (LiDAR) data collected in 2008 would facilitate hydraulic and sediment-transport modeling and characterization of bar elevations throughout most of the study area.

- Few studies describing channel morphology and sediment transport exist for the Hunter Creek basin. The most detailed study reported channel incision and bank instability as well as the loss of point bars and pools in the lower 3.9 km of Hunter Creek from slightly downstream of its confluence with Yorke Creek to its mouth (EA Engineering, Science, and Technology, 1998).

1

- Repeat channel cross-sections collected from 1994 to 2010 at four bridges indicate that Hunter Creek is dynamic and subject to channel shifting, aggradation, and incision. Despite this dynamism, the channel at three bridge crossings showed little net change in thalweg elevation during this period. However, the channel thalweg aggraded 0.55 m from 2004 to 2008 near the bridge at RKM 3.5.

- Systematic delineation of gravel bars from aerial photographs collected in 1940, 1965, 2005, and 2009 indicates a 52-percent reduction in the area of bed-material sediment throughout the study area from 1940 to 2009. Net bar loss was greatest in the Lower Study Reach from RKM 1–4 and mainly is associated with the encroachment of vegetation onto upper-bar surfaces lacking apparent vegetation in 1940.

- Bar-surface material was approximately equal in size to bar-subsurface material at Conn Creek Bar, whereas it was distinctly coarser than the subsurface material at Menasha Bar. Armoring ratios, which indicate the coarseness of the bar surface relative to the bar subsurface, were calculated as 0.97 for Conn Creek Bar and 1.5 for Menasha Bar. These ratios tentatively show that transport capacity and sediment supply are relatively balanced at these sites.

- On the basis of datasets reviewed in this reconnaissance-level study, study results indicate that (1) the size and overall position of gravel bars in the lower 12.4 km of Hunter Creek are determined largely by valley physiography such that unconfined alluvial sections have large channel-flanking bars, whereas confined reaches accommodate only relatively smaller bars, (2) the alluvial segments are prone to vertical and lateral channel adjustments, (3) substantial aggradation or incision did not occur except near RKM 3.5, where the channel aggraded 0.55 m (meters) from 2004 to 2008,

and (4) bed-material transport in Hunter Creek is tentatively considered unlimited relative to sediment supply.

- Study findings indicate that more detailed investigations are needed to assess channel condition in the Lower Study Reach as well as longitudinal trends in particle size, the relative balance between sediment supply and transport capacity, and potential drivers of bar area loss (such as vegetation encroachment and peak-flow patterns) throughout the study area.

Introduction

This report summarizes a reconnaissance-level assessment of channel condition and bed-material transport relevant to the permitting of instream gravel extraction in Hunter Creek, a coastal stream draining to the Pacific Ocean south of Gold Beach, Oregon (fig. 1, next page). The assessment is based on a review of existing datasets (such as bridge-inspection surveys, watershed analyses, and gravel-extraction records), repeat delineation of bar and channel features from aerial photographs, and field observations and particle-size measurements made during July 2010. Findings from these multiple datasets and observations were used to (1) assess the vertical stability of the Hunter Creek channel and identify locations where the channel may be incising, aggrading, or stable and (2) identify key datasets and issues that are relevant to understanding channel condition, bed-material transport, and potential effects of instream gravel extraction on Hunter Creek. Overall, this preliminary study constitutes a ―Phase I‖ investigation, similar to the Umpqua Phase I assessment by O'Connor and others (2009), as outlined by the U.S. Army Corps of Engineers, Portland District, and the Oregon Department of State Lands to inform the permitting of instream gravel extraction in Oregon.

Location References

Locations along Hunter Creek are referenced to river kilometers (RKM) that begin at the Highway 101 bridge, which is less than 200 m upstream from the mouth of Hunter Creek at the Pacific Ocean. To develop this linear-reference system, (fig. 1) a centerline was digitized through the wetted channel of Hunter Creek for the entire study area from orthoimagery collected in 2009 by the National Agriculture Imagery Program (NAIP). Points were then distributed at 0.2-km intervals along this centerline and used to determine locations in terms of river kilometer for this project. Even after accounting for the conversion between river miles (RM)

shown on current (1986) U.S. Geological Survey (USGS) quadrangle maps and river kilometers produced by this study for Hunter Creek, the two reference systems differ owing to factors such as some channel shifting. Additionally, USGS quadrangles of the Hunter Creek basin include only RM 4–7 (as indicated in fig. 1).

Physical Characteristics of the Hunter Creek Basin

Geographic, Geologic, and Geomorphic Setting

Hunter Creek is an unregulated system that drains 115 km^2 of southwestern Oregon before flowing into the Pacific Ocean south of the town of Gold Beach, Oregon (fig. 1). The basin is located wholly within Curry County. The drainage basin is flanked to the north by the Rogue River basin, to the east by the Illinois River basin, and to the south by the Pistol River basin. The main stem and its four principal tributaries (North Fork Hunter Creek, Big South Fork Hunter Creek, Little South Fork Hunter Creek, and Conn Creek) drain the rugged Klamath Mountains, which are underlain by a Cretaceous and Jurassic accretionary complex composed of weakly to intensely metamorphosed sedimentary, volcanic, and intrusive igneous rocks (Ramp and others, 1977).

The headwaters of Hunter Creek begin near Sugarloaf Mountain (peak elevation 1,017 m) in the Rogue River–Siskiyou National Forest. Hunter Creek then flows generally westward for 14 km before its confluence with the higher gradient North Fork Hunter Creek (drainage area of 15.4 km^2) (figs. 1 and 2A). The channel within this uppermost portion of the drainage basin is steep (gradient of 0.049 m/m; as measured from a 10-m USGS Digital Elevation Model [DEM], fig. 2A) and carves a narrow canyon through Cretaceous-age Colebrook Schist and partially metamorphosed sedimentary rocks of the Jurassic-age Dothan and Otter Point Formations (fig. 1).

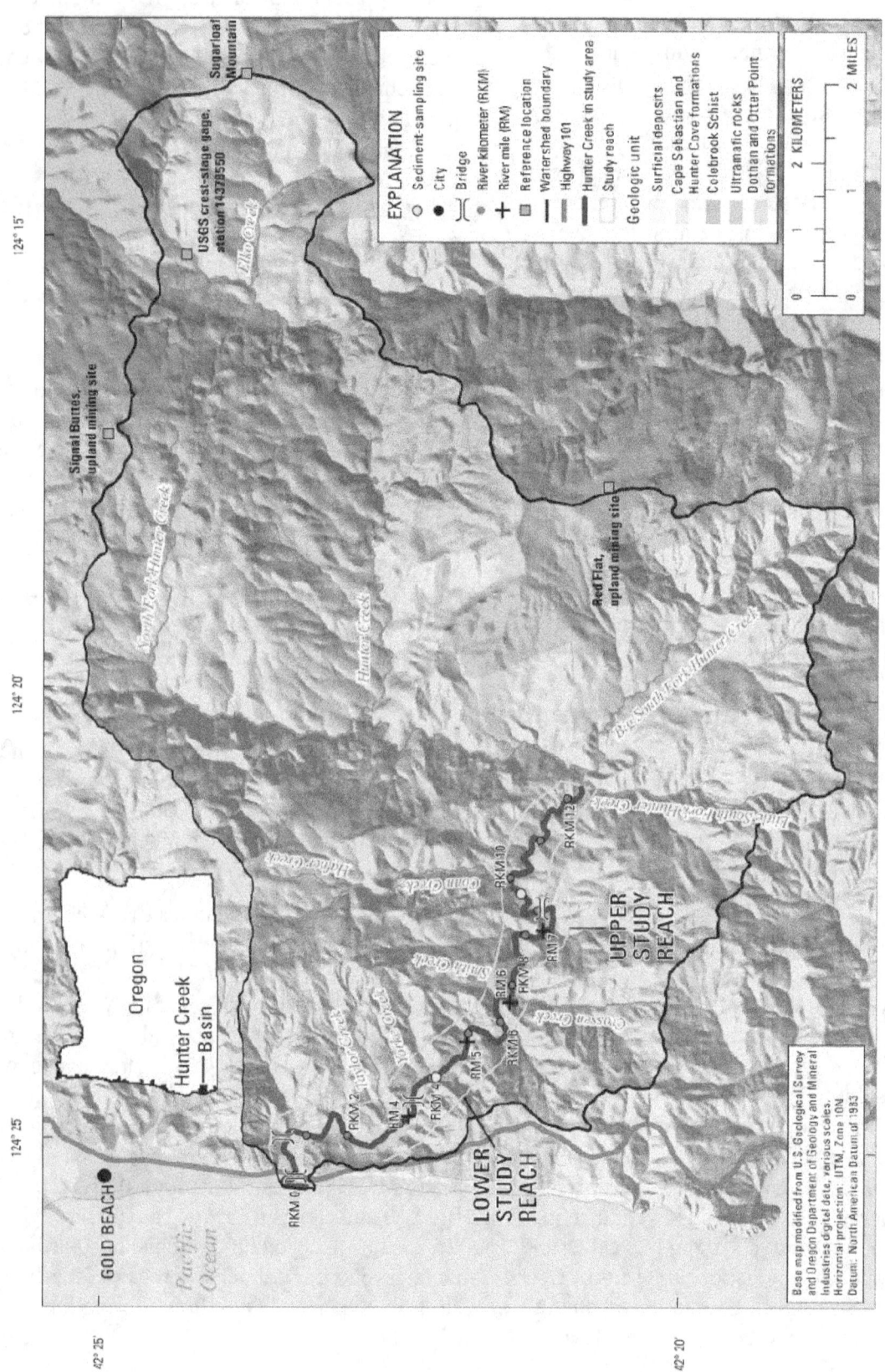

Figure 1. Map of the Hunter Creek basin, southwestern Oregon. River kilometer (RKM) locations were derived by this project (see Location References section for details); river mile (RM) locations were derived from U.S. Geological Survey quadrangle maps.

In the 2009 NAIP orthoimagery of the basin, the main channel in the upper 14 km of the basin is narrow and completely obscured by adjacent tree canopies except for in landslide-prone areas that are dominated by Jurassic and Cretaceous ultramafic rocks. Within these unstable segments, the channel widens to approximately 12 m (as measured from 2009 NAIP orthoimagery for this and all widths provided in this section), accommodating numerous channel-flanking gravel bars.

About 3.5 km above its confluence with North Fork Hunter Creek, Hunter Creek exits the ultramafic rock formations and enters the Dothan and Otter Point Formations that underlay the middle and lower portions of the drainage basin (fig. 1). Downstream of this confluence, Hunter Creek flows southward for 5 km until it is joined by Big South Fork Hunter Creek (15.7 km^2) and shortly thereafter by Little South Fork Hunter Creek (6.8 km^2) (fig. 1). Within this middle portion of the drainage basin, the channel widens to nearly 25 m, decreases in gradient to 0.021 m/m (fig. 2A), and flows on a mixed bed of boulders and bedrock with intermittent gravel bars positioned at high-amplitude bends. At its confluence with Little South Fork Hunter Creek, the drainage area of Hunter Creek is 82.6 km^2.

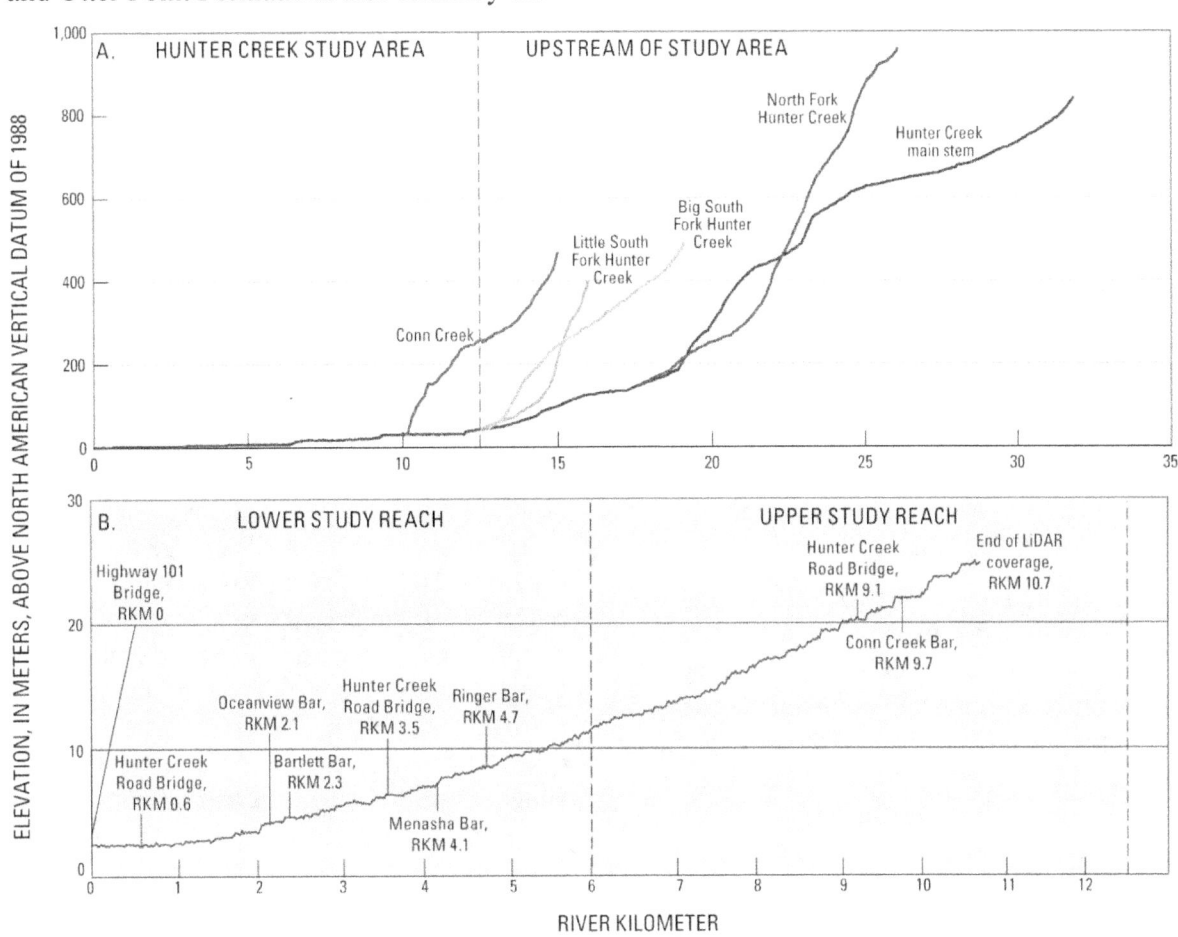

Figure 2. Longitudinal profiles for (A) the Hunter Creek basin, southwestern Oregon (as measured from U.S. Geological Survey 10-meter Digital Elevation Model) and (B) study area (as measured from 1-meter LiDAR survey), with locations of sediment-sampling sites and bridges denoted.

From its confluence with Little South Fork Hunter Creek to 1.4 km downstream, the Hunter Creek channel is confined by a bedrock-dominated canyon and flows over a mixed bed of bedrock, boulders, and gravel. The lower 11 km of Hunter Creek flows northwest towards its mouth at the Pacific Ocean as a ¬wandering gravel bed river" (Church, 1983) dominated by a single channel with some multichanneled reaches. The active channel in this lowermost 11 km primarily is alluvial and flanked by nearly continuous swaths of large, active gravel bars that are separated by several 1–2 km confined reaches (figs. 1 and 3A–D). Within the unconfined segments, the channel generally contains large gravel bars and alternates its position between valley walls, forming shallow riffles where it crosses the valley floor and deep pools where it flows against valley walls. The main tributary in this section is Conn Creek (6.0 km^2), which enters Hunter Creek approximately 2.5 km downstream from its confluence with Little South Fork Hunter Creek (fig. 1). The channel in the lower 10.7 km of Hunter Creek has an average gradient of 0.002 m/m (as measured from a 1-m LiDAR survey; fig. 2B) and a wetted width ranging from 15 m in the confined, upper portion of the study area to nearly 165 m near the mouth. Hunter Creek is tidally influenced in approximately its lowest 2.2 km.

The longitudinal profile (fig. 2A–B) shows a smooth gradation in slope along Hunter Creek to its confluence with the Pacific Ocean. This profile, together with abundant gravel bars observed to the mouth and the absence of an estuary, indicates that Hunter Creek has transported gravel to the Pacific Ocean at a rate that has exceeded the depositional accommodation space created by Holocene sea-level rise and hence differs from many Coast Range drainages where extensive tidal reaches and fluvial estuaries occur (Komar, 1997). The wide valley bottom in the lowest portion of the study area, in part, reflects Holocene filling of the Hunter Creek valley.

Hydrology

The hydrology of Hunter Creek is not systematically monitored by any existing local or Federal program. The only discharge data for the Hunter Creek basin are provided by a USGS crest-stage station (14378550), which was operated from water years 1965–1977 on Hunter Creek upstream of its confluence with Elko Creek (fig. 1). This crest-stage station provides the date and magnitude of annual peak flows during its period of operation.

Since bed-material transport is determined largely by the magnitude and frequency of high-flow events, this project compiled existing information for the Hunter Creek basin and nearby basins and estimated peak flow for a range of discharge events on Hunter Creek (tables 1 and 2). Unlike nearby higher elevation basins, where peak flows derive from rain-on-snow events (such as the Illinois River; mean basin elevation 814 m), peak flows in Hunter Creek (mean basin elevation 466 m) derive mainly from large frontal rainstorms because only 15 percent of the basin is within the transient snow zone (EA Engineering, Science, and Technology, 1998). Streamflow typically peaks during the rainy winter season and recedes to base flow (or periods of no flow) during the late summer, when precipitation is scarce. Peak-flow discharge was estimated for 2-, 5-, 10-, 25-, 50-, 100-, and 500-year recurrence-interval events at three locations by using regional-regression relationships developed by Cooper (2005): the former site of the USGS crest-stage station in the upper watershed, Hunter Creek at its confluence with Little South Fork Hunter Creek (near the upstream boundary of the study area), and Hunter Creek at its mouth (table 1).

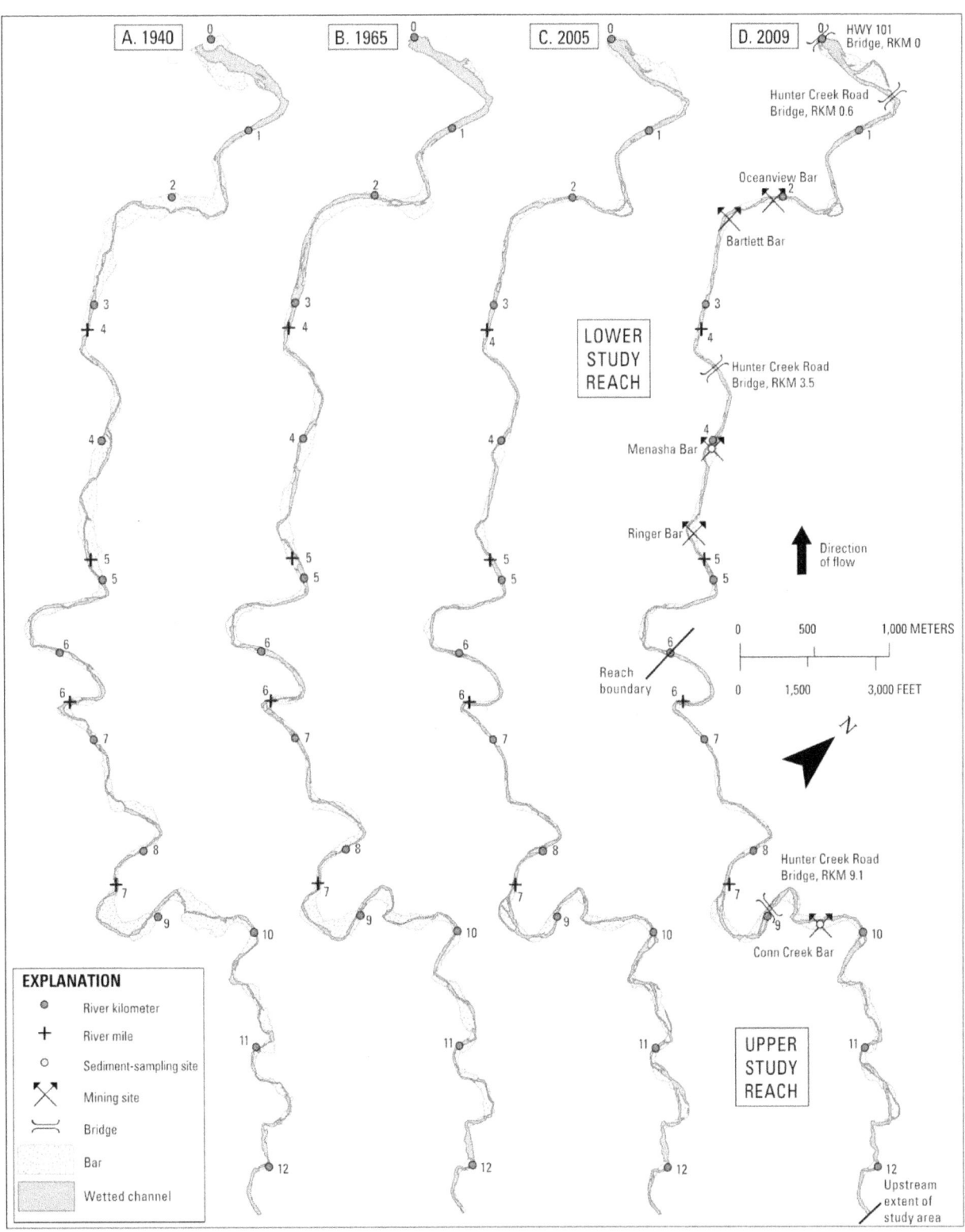

Figure 3. Gravel bars and wetted channel as delineated for the study reaches on Hunter Creek, southwestern Oregon, in (A) 1940, (B) 1965, (C) 2005, and (D) 2009. Locations of sediment-sampling sites, bridges, and historical and ongoing instream gravel extraction sites are indicated on (D).

Table 1. Estimated peak flows at sites in the Hunter Creek basin, southwestern Oregon.

[m^3/s, cubic meter per second; km^2, square kilometer; peak flows estimated using regional regression equations from Cooper (2005); basin area from StreamStats (*http://streamstatsags.cr.usgs.gov*)]

U.S. Geological Survey crest-stage site (14378550) on Hunter Creek near Gold Beach, Oregon

Basin drainage area: 2.51 km²

Recurrence interval (years)	Flow (m³/s)	Prediction error (percent)[1]	Equivalent years of record[2]	90-percent prediction interval	
				Lower (m³/s)	Upper (m³/s)
2	3.68	27	2.4	2.37	5.72
5	5.61	25	3.7	3.68	8.49
10	6.94	26	5.0	4.56	10.6
25	8.78	27	6.4	5.66	13.6
50	10.2	28	7.2	6.46	16.1
100	11.7	29	7.9	7.22	18.8
500	15.2	33	8.9	8.92	26.0

Hunter Creek at its confluence with the Little South Fork Hunter Creek

Basin drainage area: 82.6 km²

Recurrence interval (years)	Flow (m³/s)	Prediction error (percent)[1]	Equivalent years of record[2]	90-percent prediction interval	
				Lower (m³/s)	Upper (m³/s)
2	110	27	2.4	71.1	170
5	161	25	3.7	107	243
10	195	26	5.0	129	294
25	240	27	6.4	156	368
50	274	28	7.2	175	428
100	309	29	7.9	193	496
500	391	33	8.9	231	660

Hunter Creek at its mouth

Basin drainage area: 115 km²

Recurrence interval (years)	Flow (m³/s)	Prediction error (percent)[1]	Equivalent years of record[2]	90-Percent prediction interval	
				Lower (m³/s)	Upper (m³/s)
2	142	27	2.4	91.5	219
5	206	25	3.7	136	311
10	248	26	5.0	164	377
25	303	27	6.4	197	467
50	345	28	7.2	221	544
100	388	29	7.9	242	626
500	490	33	8.9	289	830

[1] Square root of the sum of the squared standard error of the model and the average squared standard error of the sampling, in log units (Cooper, 2005).

[2] Number of years of data needed to give the same average prediction error as the regression model (Cooper, 2005).

The estimated peak-flow discharges reflect the small size of the Hunter Creek watershed (table 1). For example, the 2-year flood discharge at the mouth of Hunter Creek is approximately 142 m^3/s, with a 90-percent prediction interval ranging from 91.5 to 219 m^3/s (table 1). The 90-percent prediction intervals for the 10- and 100-year recurrence-interval floods at the mouth of Hunter Creek are 164–377 m^3/s and 242–626 m^3/s, respectively (table 1). Comparison of estimated peak flows for Hunter Creek and five nearby USGS streamflow stations in basins of varying size show that regional flooding is localized (table 2). For example, during the large magnitude rain-on-snow flood of December 1964 (water year 1965), discharge on the Illinois and Chetco Rivers exceeded the 500- and 100-year recurrence intervals, respectively (table 2). Similarly, peak flow for water year 1965 at the USGS crest-stage in the upper Hunter Creek basin was greater than the weighted peak flow for a 500-year recurrence-interval flood (table 2).

Despite large uncertainties in the weighted peak-flow estimates (Cooper, 2005), flooding during the December 1964 flood in the upper Hunter Creek basin may not be representative of overall watershed conditions. Harris Creek (a coastal basin north of the Chetco River) and Ransom Creek (a tributary to the lower Chetco River) are both relatively small, low-elevation basins that experienced a less than 2-year recurrence-interval event during the December 1964 storm (table 2). The lower Hunter Creek channel may have responded similarly with relatively low flow during this storm. Further hydrologic analyses that estimate the historical peak flows in lower Hunter Creek may help better quantify the hydrologic response of the basin to peak-flow events.

Land Uses in the Basin

The Hunter Creek Watershed Assessment (Maguire, 2001) and Hunter Creek Watershed Analysis (EA Engineering, Science, and Technology, 1998) summarize land-use activities in the basin. Like other basins along the southwestern Oregon coast, Euro-American settlement of the Hunter Creek basin was fueled by the discovery of gold in the nearby Rogue River basin and elsewhere along the Oregon coast during the 1850s. The population of the Hunter Creek basin grew slowly during the 19th and early 20th centuries and remains sparse today, owing in part to the limited amount of arable land along Hunter Creek and its remote location. When the lower portion of the Hunter Creek basin was annexed into the City of Gold Beach in 1995, the area had an estimated population of only 414 (Maguire, 2001). Another impediment to basinwide development was the lack of roads. Until the end of World War II, the primary transportation routes connecting the coast and upper watershed were trails carved along steep hill slopes and the river bed during low flows (Maguire, 2001).

The watershed-scale activities that likely have had the greatest effect on channel morphology in Hunter Creek are timber harvesting and associated road building. In 2001, private and Federal forest lands accounted for 97 percent of the basin area; urban, agricultural, and rural-residential areas along the lower main stem accounted for the remaining 3 percent (Maguire, 2001). EA Engineering, Science, and Technology (1998) reported that commercial timber harvest began in the late 1940s, peaked from 1955 to 1964, with logging mainly on privately owned lands, and then went through a second period of substantial harvest from 1980 to 1989, when the Rogue River–Siskiyou National Forest lands were timbered. Prior to timber harvest, the main watershed disturbances were fire and large wind-throw events (EA Engineering, Science, and Technology, 1998); no fires have occurred during the modern period of record (Peck and Park, 2006).

Table 2. Peak-flow characteristics at U.S. Geological Survey streamflow sites within or near the Hunter Creek basin, southwestern Oregon.

[m, meter; mm, millimeter; km², square kilometer; RI, recurrence interval in years; >, greater than; <, less than; NA, not available; flows in cubic meters per second; estimated peak flows are weighted using regional regressions and station data from Appendix D, Cooper, 2005; mean basin elevation, mean annual precipitation, and basin area from StreamStats (*http://streamstatsags.cr.usgs.gov*)]

Station number	Station name	Unregulated period used in peak-flow analysis[1]	Mean basin elevation[1] (m)	Mean annual precipitation[1] (mm)	Basin area[1] (km²)	Weighted[2] peak flows for indicated recurrence intervals (m³/s)							Measured annual peak flows			
													Water year 1965		Water year 1997	
						2	5	10	25	50	100	500	Flow	RI	Flow	RI
14372300	Rogue River near Agness	1961–1976	930	1,052	10,205	2,888	4,870	6,286	8,155	9,599	11,100	14,866	8,212	>25	NA[3]	NA
14377100	Illinois River near Kerby	1962–1999[4]	881	1,918	987	677	937	1,116	1,345	1,521	1,702	2,135	2,611	>500	1,059	<10
14378550	Hunter Creek near Gold Beach	1965–1977	850	3,785	3	6	8	9	11	12	14	18	25	>500	NA	NA
14378800	Harris Creek near Brookings	1953–1968	184	2,281	3	5	7	9	11	12	14	18	3	<2	NA	NA
14378900	Ransom Creek near Brookings	1953–1977	123	2,078	2	3	5	6	8	9	11	14	2	<2	NA	NA
14400000	Chetco River near Brookings	1965; 1970–2000[4]	671	3,099	702	1,022	1,413	1,656	1,954	2,166	2,373	2,832	2,418	>100	2,155	<50

[1] Reported values for basin elevation, precipitation, and area refer to contributing watershed for each gaging station, not basin outlet.

[2] Weighted peak flows incorporate both historical station data and calculated peak flows from regional regressions. Weighted peak flows differ from values in table 1, which are based solely on regional regression formulas.

[3] Flow in water year 1997 affected by regulation.

[4] Although Illinois and Chetco Rivers currently (2011) are unregulated, the peak-flow values provided in this table are based on estimates from Cooper (2005), which incorporate data only up to 1999 and 2000, respectively.

The Hunter Creek basin also has a history of mining that likely has affected channel morphology and bed-material transport. In the 1850s, placer deposits near the mouth of Hunter Creek and nearby terraces were mined briefly for gold (EA Engineering, Science, and Technology, 1998). On the basis of historical mining practices in other coastal basins, like the Umpqua River basin (Beckham, 1986), placer deposits in Hunter Creek may have been extracted hydraulically, potentially liberating large volumes of sediment from streamside terraces. Since at least the 1960s, commercial aggregate has been extracted from gravel bars along the lower 10 km of Hunter Creek (on the basis of data provided by Dan Crumley, Curry County Road Department, written commun., 2010). Because instream gravel extraction can result in channel incision and bar armoring (Kondolf, 1994), extraction volumes and gravel replenishment at mining sites are described in more detail in a subsequent section of this report. Other mining activities include commercial exploration and mining in the 1930s–1950s for nickel, gold, and chromite deposits in the upper watershed near Signal Buttes and Red Flat (fig. 1). These activities probably had a minimal impact on Hunter Creek channel morphology because they were located more than 5 km from the main channel and mainly involved trenching and prospecting rather than large-scale extraction (EA Engineering, Science, and Technology, 1998; Maguire, 2001). Aggregate continues to be extracted in the uplands of the basin.

The morphology of the lower 3.9 km of Hunter Creek (from below its confluence with Yorke Creek to its mouth) has been directly affected by channel straightening and bank armoring undertaken by local entities to protect properties and road infrastructure as well as floodplain reclamation (EA Engineering, Science, and Technology, 1998). Completed in the mid-1940s, Hunter Creek Road generally follows the lower 13 km of Hunter Creek and impinges upon the historical active channel in several locations, such as near RKM 4.5, 7.6, and 9.6.

Study Area

For the purposes of this reconnaissance study, the study area includes the lower 12.4 km of Hunter Creek from its confluence with the Little South Fork Hunter Creek at RKM 12.4 to near its mouth at the Highway 101 bridge (figs. 1 and 3A–D). This predominately alluvial stretch of river contains most of the gravel bars in the basin and all instream gravel-extraction operations active in 2010. This study area was further subdivided into two study reaches (Upper Study Reach and Lower Study Reach) based primarily on valley morphology (table 3 and fig. 3A–D).

The Upper Study Reach spans the upper 6.5 km of Hunter Creek from RKM 12.4 near its confluence with Little South Fork Hunter Creek to RKM 6.0 near its confluences with Crossen and Smith Creeks (figs. 1 and 3A–D). In the uppermost 1.4 km of the Upper Study Reach, the channel is confined by a narrow, bedrock-dominated canyon. Here, active channel width, or the area typically inundated during annual high flows as determined by the presence of water and flow-modified surfaces (Church, 1988), ranges from 12 to 20 m (as measured from 2009 NAIP orthoimagery for this and all widths reported in this section). The bedrock canyon at the upstream boundary of the study area would prevent any channel changes in the study area from propagating upstream. Downstream from RKM 11, the valley in the Upper Study Reach opens, allowing the active channel to widen 40 to 75 m and transition into a fully alluvial segment with a pool-drop morphology and large channel-flanking gravel bars. Near RKM 8.4, the channel enters a second confined segment that extends to RKM 6, where the active channel width is less than 30 m but fully alluvial. The average water-surface gradient of the Upper Study Reach is 0.009 m/m (as measured from LiDAR data collected from RKM 6 to 10.7; fig. 2B and table 3).

The Lower Study Reach begins at RKM 6 at the outlet of a confined segment and extends to RKM 0 at the Highway 101 bridge (figs. 1 and 3A–D). Although alternating bars are present throughout this reach, the Lower Study Reach has broad, unconfined segments with active-channel widths up to 80 m (such as near RKM 4.1 and 4.6) as well as a narrower, confined active-channel segment where the maximum width generally is less than 35 m (such as near RKM 2.6–3.9). Near RKM 0.6, Hunter Creek abruptly turns westward across its coastal plain and widens to 165 m as it flows towards its mouth at the Pacific Ocean. The average water-surface gradient for the Lower Study Reach is 0.005 m/m (fig. 2B and table 3).

Table 3. Summary of characteristics for the study reaches in the Hunter Creek basin, southwestern Oregon.

[RKM, river kilometer; km^2, square kilometer; m, meter; km, kilometer; LiDAR, Light Detection And Ranging]

Attribute	Lower Study Reach	Upper Study Reach
Position	RKM 0–6	RKM 6–12.4
Reach and channel description	Alternating confined and unconfined segments. Unconfined segments have large, channel-flanking bars whereas confined, narrow segments have smaller bars. Tidally affected to about RKM 2.2. Dynamic mouth frequently changes position. Gravel and some sand bars are present in reach.	Uppermost 1.4 km confined and bedrock dominated with little gravel. Channel from RKM 8.4 to 11 is unconfined with large gravel bars and has pool-riffle morphology. Channel from RKM 6 to 8.4 is confined to narrow canyon and has smaller bars.
Area of downstream end of segment (km^2)[1]	115.0	102.0
Area at upstream end of segment (km^2)[1]	102.0	82.6
Average water-surface gradient (m/m)[2]	0.005	0.009
Major flow factors	Tidally affected to ~ RKM 2.2; minimal irrigation diversions	No regulation
Major sedimentation factors	Low gradient in unconfined segments promotes sediment deposition. Placer mining in 1850s near mouth of channel; historical and ongoing in-stream gravel extraction; forestry practices in upper basin.	Low gradient in unconfined segments promotes sediment deposition; historical and ongoing instream gravel extraction; forestry practices in upper basin; sediment inputs from the Little and Big South Forks of Hunter Creek and Conn Creek.
Direct impacts to active channel	Gravel mining; recreational vehicle use; channel straightening and bank armoring in lower 3.9 km; placer mining in 1850s.	Gravel mining; recreational vehicle use
General channel trends	Channel flows on alluvium and historically has been dynamic, particularly near river's mouth.	Upper 1.4 km historically stable due to bedrock influence. Channel from RKM 6 to 11 mainly flows on alluvium and has been more historically dynamic and subject to shifting.

[1] Basin area for the total contributing area from StreamStats (http://streamstatsags.cr.usgs.gov).

[2] Water-surface gradient extracted from 2008 LiDAR survey encompassing RKM 0–10.7; therefore, gradient for Upper Study Reach was determined only for RKM 6–10.7.

Approach and Key Findings

For this study, we reviewed existing datasets and studies regarding channel condition and bed-material transport in the Hunter Creek basin, applied reconnaissance-level GIS analyses, and collected field observations and particle-size measurements during July 2010. The objectives of these efforts were to (1) identify existing datasets that would support more detailed analyses of bed-material transport and channel condition, (2) summarize instream gravel-extraction activities, (3) characterize broad-scale patterns in gravel-bar area and channel features using four sets of aerial photographs spanning 1940–2009, (4) determine particle-size distributions and armoring ratios on two gravel bars, and (5) identify locations where the channel may be aggrading or incising. Additionally, this assessment provides a preliminary review of channel condition and bed-material transport in Hunter Creek and identifies outstanding issues relevant to the permitting of instream gravel extraction that may be addressed by future studies. The following sections summarize each of the major activities and key findings.

Review of Previous Hydrologic and Geomorphic Studies

Two watershed-scale assessments provide information on the hydrology and geomorphology of Hunter Creek. The Hunter Creek Watershed Assessment (Maguire, 2001) provides general information on basin hydrology and land-use while the Hunter Creek Watershed Analysis (EA Engineering, Science, and Technology, 1998), which also is summarized by Peck and Park (2006), provides a more detailed description of erosion processes throughout the basin.

Based on EA Engineering, Science, and Technology (1998), sources of sediment to Hunter Creek and its tributaries primarily are mass movements with smaller inputs contributed by surface erosion associated with road networks and skids trails at logging sites. Throughout much of the upper and middle portions of the Hunter Creek basin, the channel flows directly on bedrock and is relatively stable (EA Engineering, Science, and Technology, 1998). The main areas of Hunter Creek prone to channel instability are in (1) portions of the upper basin and Elko Creek where the channel flows adjacent to unstable, landslide-prone slopes derived from ultramafic rocks and (2) lower, alluvial reaches where stream banks are composed of alluvium and subject to erosion (EA Engineering, Science, and Technology, 1998). Additionally, they reported incision along the lower 3.9 km of Hunter Creek as well as channel straightening, bank failures, and loss of point bars and pools; these changes were attributed to bank stabilization and floodplain reclamation (EA Engineering, Science, and Technology, 1998).

The finding of incision by EA Engineering, Science, and Technology (1998) is particularly relevant to this study since documentation of incision or aggradation is a major focus of Phase I analyses (Janine Castro, U.S. Fish and Wildlife Service, written commun., 2006). Field visits and interviews are cited as evidence for channel incision (p. 4–25; EA, Engineering, Science, and Technology, 1998). As described in subsequent sections, our limited review of quantitative data describing channel elevation does not indicate systematic channel incision since 1994.

Assessment of Existing Spatial Datasets

We assessed the availability of spatial datasets in the Hunter Creek basin that could be used to evaluate channel condition and bed-material transport. This search focused primarily on aerial photographs and included other datasets such as Light Detection And Ranging (LiDAR), geologic maps, General Land Office (GLO) surveys, and navigation surveys.

This project included the review of aerial photographs of the Hunter Creek basin available from the U.S. Army Corps of Engineers' Aerial Photograph Library (Portland, Oregon) and the University of Oregon Map Library (Eugene, Oregon) as well as digital orthophotographs available from online sources (table 4). Other potential sources of aerial photographs not considered in this review include (but are not limited to) the Bureau of Land Management, National Archives, Curry County departments, and South Coast Lumber Company.

On the basis of the aerial photography review, at least 12 sets of aerial photographs are available that cover all or most of the 12.4-km long Hunter Creek study area (table 4). Complete photographic coverage for the study area is available at least once per decade since the 1940s. Six additional sets of photographs partially cover the study area, four of which completely capture the Lower Study Reach. A majority of the identified sets of photographs were taken at a sufficient resolution (1:24,000 or greater) for assessing long-term changes in channel condition, gravel-bar area, and vegetation cover.

The earliest available surveys of the Hunter Creek study area were conducted by the GLO in 1857 and produced as maps in 1881 and 1891 (table 4). As summarized by Atwood (2008), the main purpose of GLO surveys was to establish the Township, Range, and Section lines of the Public Land Survey System (PLSS). Since these maps were based on non-meandered surveys, the approximate location of Hunter Creek is depicted in the GLO maps, but specific features such as gravel bars were not systematically mapped and channel banks were not continuously surveyed. Further review of the GLO data would help determine if surveyors recorded any relevant descriptions of channel and vegetation conditions in their notes.

Other spatial datasets include a LiDAR survey that provides high resolution (1-m scale) topographic data for the river corridor from RKM 0 to 10.7 (table 4). This dataset, collected in 2008 would support detailed analyses of channel hydraulics and sediment transport. Topography data at a coarser scale (10-m) are available for the entire watershed (table 4). Also available is the geologic map of Curry County developed by Ramp and others (1977), which depicts major geologic units and geomorphic divisions of the river basin (table 4 and fig. 1). Our preliminary search for navigation reports and surveys did not yield any results, which is reasonable given the minimal size of the estuary, lack of navigation improvements such as jetties, and the dynamic river mouth that shifts position frequently (fig. 3A–D).Furthermore, Farnell (1981) states that in Curry County, "only on the Chetco River was there sufficient commercial use to warrant a claim by the State to the bed of the river" for navigation purposes.

Table 4. List of spatial datasets reviewed during this study for the Hunter Creek study area, southwestern Oregon

[USFS, U.S. Forest Service; UO, University of Oregon; USGS, U.S. Geological Survey; SCS, Soil Conservation Service; Oregon DOR, Oregon Department of Revenue; WAC, Western Aerial Contractor; USACE, U.S. Army Corps of Engineers; BLM, Bureau of Land Management; m, meter; NAIP, National Agriculture Imagery Program; NA, not available; LiDAR, Light Detection And Ranging; DOGAMI, Oregon Department of Geology and Mineral Industries; DEM, digital elevation model; NED, National Elevation Dataset; aerial photographs noted in **bold** were used to delineate gravel-bar features for this project]

Data type	Year[1]	Area covered[2]	Scale	Source	Flight date(s)	Current location
Aerial photographs and orthophotos	**1940**	**Full coverage**	**1:20,000**	**USFS**	**8/3/1940; 10/14/1941**	**UO Library**
	1952	Full coverage	1:47,200	USGS		UO Library
	1965	**Full coverage**	**1:20,000**	**SCS**	**6/22/1965; 8/13/1965**	**UO Library**
	1970	Full coverage	1:12,000	Oregon DOR		UO Library
	1983	Full coverage	1:48,000	WAC		USACE, Portland District
	1986	Full coverage	1:12,000	BLM		USGS; UO Library
	1995	Full coverage	1 pixel = 1 m	USGS		UO Library; USGS, *http://edcsns17.cr.usgs.gov/NewEarthExplorer/*
	2000	Full coverage	1 pixel = 1 m	USGS		USGS, *http://edcsns17.cr.usgs.gov/NewEarthExplorer/*
	2002	Full coverage	1:12,000	BLM		UO Library
	2005	**Full coverage**	**1 pixel = 0.5 m**	**NAIP**	**7/17/2005**	**USGS;** ***http://datagateway.nrcs.usda.gov/***
	2009	**Full coverage**	**1 pixel = 1 m**	**NAIP**	**6/17/2009**	**USGS;** ***http://datagateway.nrcs.usda.gov/***
	1962	RKM 0–2.6	1:12,000	NA		USACE, Portland District
	1964	RKM 0–10.8	1:24,000	NA		USACE, Portland District
	1977	RKM 0–5.4	1:24,000	WAC		USACE, Portland District
	1980	RKM 0–8.2	1:24,000	WAC		USACE, Portland District
	1982	RKM 0–12.2	1:24,000	WAC		USACE, Portland District
	1989	RKM 0–8.2	1:48,000	USACE		USACE, Portland District
	1998	RKM 0–3.2	1:16,200	USACE		USACE, Portland District
LiDAR survey	2008	RKM 0–10.7	1 pixel = ~1 m	DOGAMI		DOGAMI
DEM	Source dates vary	Full coverage	1 pixel = 10 m	USGS NED		USGS website: *http://seamless.usgs.gov*

Table 4. List of spatial datasets reviewed during this study for the Hunter Creek study area, southwestern Oregon—continued.

[USFS, U.S. Forest Service; UO, University of Oregon; USGS, U.S. Geological Survey; SCS, Soil Conservation Service; Oregon DOR, Oregon Department of Revenue; WAC, Western Aerial Contractor; USACE, U.S. Army Corps of Engineers; BLM, Bureau of Land Management; m, meter; NAIP, National Agriculture Imagery Program; NA, not available; LiDAR, Light Detection And Ranging; DOGAMI, Oregon Department of Geology and Mineral Industries; DEM, digital elevation model; NED, National Elevation Dataset; aerial photographs noted in **bold** were used to delineate gravel-bar features for this project]

Data type	Year[1]	Area covered[2]	Scale	Source	Flight date(s)	Current location
Geologic map of Curry County	1977	Full coverage	1:125,000	DOGAMI; Ramp and others (1977)		DOGAMI
General Land Office surveys	Surveyed in 1857; maps completed in 1881 and 1891	Full coverage	1:31,680	BLM		BLM website: *http://www.blm.gov/or/landrecords/survey/ySrvy1.php*

[1] Actual acquisition dates vary and may include multiple years.

[2] The provided spatial extent is approximate for datasets with partial coverage.

Review of Gravel-Operator Information and Surveys

In 2004, Curry County Department of Public Services inventoried instream gravel-removal permits issued in the county since 1972 (Pratt, 2004) and documented permits issued within the Hunter Creek basin during this period. In 1972, eight permits with a total annual-removal limit of approximately 52,750 m^3 were issued along Hunter Creek for primarily highway and county-road maintenance, flood prevention, and commercial uses (Pratt, 2004). The number of active instream gravel-removal permits decreased to five by 2004 with a total annual-removal volume limit of approximately 30,580 m^3. The declining number of instream gravel-extraction permits on Hunter Creek mirrors the general downward trend in these permits throughout Curry County, where the number of countywide permits declined from 61 in 1972 to 19 in 2004 (Pratt, 2004).

Partial-volume estimates of gravel extracted from Hunter Creek from 1966 to 2010 were provided by the Curry County Road Department (table 5; Dan Crumley, Curry County Road Department, written commun., 2010). Although gaps within the record preclude a full accounting of the total volume mined from all sites, annual instream gravel-extraction volumes noted for five sites on Hunter Creek ranged from 235 to 11,808 m^3 but typically were less than 6,000 m^3 (fig. 4 and table 5). On the basis of available data, the cumulative volume of gravel removed from Hunter Creek by the Curry County Road Department from 1966 to 2010 was at least 112,612 m^3. Although unknown, the total volume of instream gravel extraction during these 44 years likely was much higher given the multiple sites operating along the river.

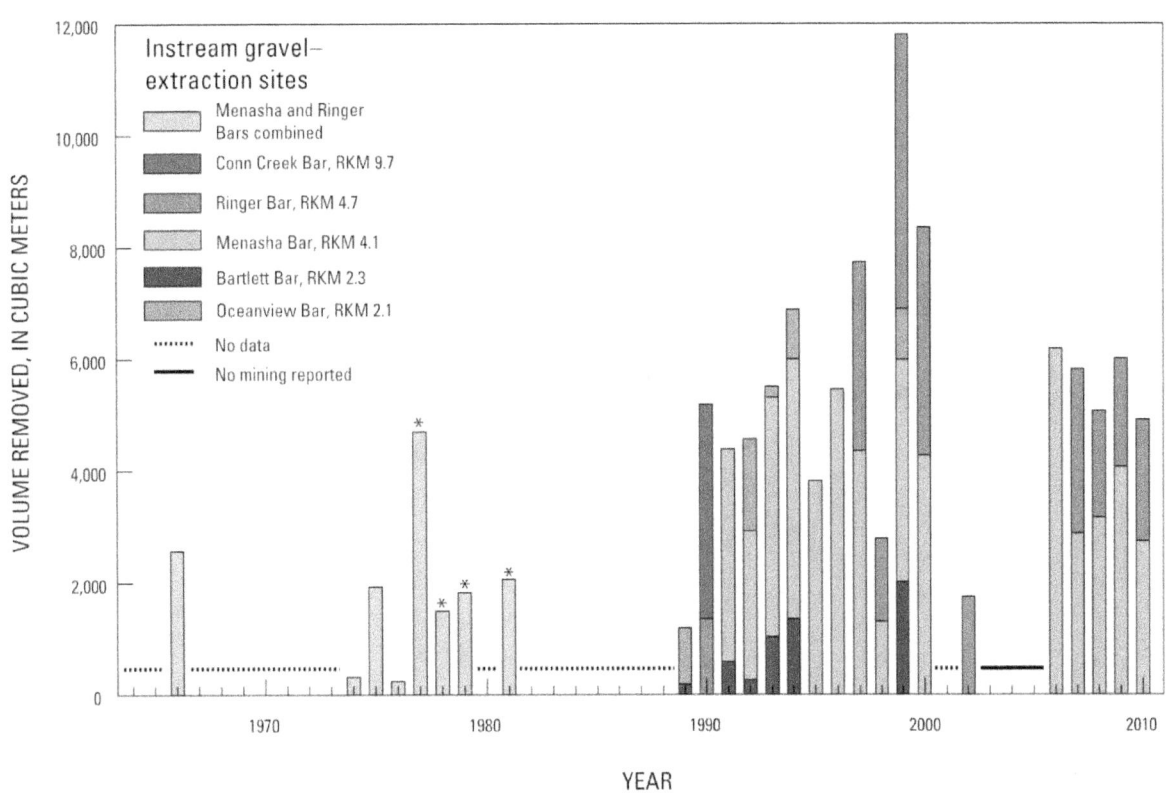

Figure 4. Partial-volume estimates of gravel extracted 1966–2010 from Hunter Creek, southwestern Oregon (data provided by Dan Crumley, Curry County Road Department, written commun., 2010). The data do not include all removal sites and years, thus they provide a minimum estimate of gravel extracted from Hunter Creek during the period. Years denoted with an asterisk had removal volumes reported by fiscal year (July 1–June 30) rather than calendar year. Approximate site location denoted by river kilometer (RKM).

Table 5. Partial compilation of instream gravel extracted from Hunter Creek, southwestern Oregon, 1966–2010

[m^3, cubic meter; RKM, river kilometer, --, data gaps; *, removal volumes provided for fiscal year, extending October 1–September 30, rather than calendar year; data provided by Dan Crumley, Curry County Road Department, written commun., 2010)]

	Gravel removed (m³) from instream extraction sites				
	Oceanview Bar	Bartlett Bar	Menasha Bar	Ringer Bar	Conn Creek Bar
Year	RKM 2.1	RKM 2.3	RKM 4.1 and 4.7 pre-1990; RKM 4.1 post-1990	RKM 4.7	RKM 9.7
1966	--	--	2,575	--	--
1967	--	--	--	--	--
1968	--	--	--	--	--
1969	--	--	--	--	--
1970	--	--	--	--	--
1971	--	--	--	--	--

17

Table 5. Partial compilation of instream gravel extracted from Hunter Creek, southwestern Oregon, 1966–2010—continued.

[m³, cubic meter; RKM, river kilometer, --, data gaps; *, removal volumes provided for fiscal year, extending October 1–September 30, rather than calendar year; data provided by Dan Crumley, Curry County Road Department, written commun., 2010)]

	Gravel removed (m³) from instream extraction sites				
	Oceanview Bar	Bartlett Bar	Menasha Bar	Ringer Bar	Conn Creek Bar
Year	RKM 2.1	RKM 2.3	RKM 4.1 and 4.7 pre-1990; RKM 4.1 post-1990	RKM 4.7	RKM 9.7
1972	--	--	--	--	--
1973	--	--	--	--	--
1974	--	--	318	--	--
1975	--	--	1,936	--	--
1976	--	--	235	--	--
1977*	--	--	4,704	--	--
1978*	--	--	1,492	--	--
1979*	--	--	1,825	--	--
1980	--	--	--	--	--
1981*	--	--	2,074	--	--
1982	--	--	--	--	--
1983	--	--	--	--	--
1984	--	--	--	--	--
1985	--	--	--	--	--
1986	--	--	--	--	--
1987	--	--	--	--	--
1988	--	--	--	--	--
1989	1,002	184	--	--	--
1990	--	--	--	1,348	3,846
1991	--	579	3,813	--	--
1992	1,634	267	2,663	--	--
1993	196	1,030	4,285	--	--
1994	894	1,353	4,641	--	--
1995	--	--	3,819	--	--
1996	--	--	5,455	--	--
1997	--	--	4,349	3,383	--
1998	--	--	1,305	1,485	--
1999	914	2,008	3,981	4,903	--
2000	Not mined	Not mined	4,270	4,086	--
2001	Not mined	Not mined	--	--	--
2002	Not mined	Not mined	Not mined	1,752	--
2003	Not mined	Not mined	Not mined	Not mined	--
2004	Not mined	Not mined	Not mined	Not mined	--

Table 5. Partial compilation of instream gravel extracted from Hunter Creek, southwestern Oregon, 1966–2010—continued.

[m³, cubic meter; RKM, river kilometer, --, data gaps; *, removal volumes provided for fiscal year, extending October 1–September 30, rather than calendar year; data provided by Dan Crumley, Curry County Road Department, written commun., 2010)]

	Gravel removed (m³) from instream extraction sites				
	Oceanview Bar	Bartlett Bar	Menasha Bar	Ringer Bar	Conn Creek Bar
Year	RKM 2.1	RKM 2.3	RKM 4.1 and 4.7 pre-1990; RKM 4.1 post-1990	RKM 4.7	RKM 9.7
2005	Not mined	Not mined	Not mined	Not mined	--
2006	Not mined	Not mined	6,186	Not mined	--
2007	Not mined	Not mined	2,875	2,942	--
2008	Not mined	Not mined	3,171	1,897	--
2009	Not mined	Not mined	4,065	1,942	--
2010	Not mined	Not mined	2,745	2,169	--

As of 2010, the three instream gravel-extraction sites active on Hunter Creek (fig. 3D) were:

- Conn Creek Bar, RKM 9.7, privately operated

- Ringer Bar, RKM 4.7, operated by Curry County Road Department

- Menasha Bar, RKM 4.1, operated by Curry County Road Department

Menasha Bar and Ringer Bar originally were privately owned, but later were acquired by Curry County Road Department in 1991 and 1989, respectively (Dan Crumley, Curry County Road Department, oral commun., 2010). These three sites have a total annual-removal limit of approximately 17,200 m³.

In Oregon, topographic surveys of sites before and after instream gravel extraction are required by regulatory agencies to document bar conditions and total removal volumes. For Hunter Creek, recent survey data were only available for Menasha and Ringer Bars (Dan Crumley, Curry County Road Department, written commun., 2010). Although no mining occurred at Menasha Bar from 2002 to 2005,

annual removal volumes ranged from 2,746 to 6,187 m³ at this site from 2006 to 2010 (fig. 4 and table 5). Likewise, Ringer Bar was not mined from 2003 to 2006, but was mined for 1,898 to 2,943 m³ of gravel from 2007 to 2010 (fig. 4 and table 5). While pre- and post-extraction surveys for the Menasha and Ringer Bars do not report annual-replenishment volumes, repeat cross-sections of the mined areas indicate that deposition during winter months rebuilds mined surfaces to approximately their pre-mining elevations. These surveys, however, also show that these sites are dynamic and subject to local scour and deposition. Therefore, a more detailed analysis of the survey data for these sites as well as the Conn Creek Bar would assist in accurately assessing bar-replenishment rates and changes in bar morphology at active instream gravel-extraction sites.

Compilation and Review of Bridge-Inspection Reports

The Oregon Department of Transportation (ODOT) conducts periodic bridge inspections to assess overall bridge condition, footing stability, and scour. Information from these assessments can be useful for evaluating channel condition. Since 1994, ODOT completed bridge-inspection reports for the following four bridges (fig. 3D) spanning the main channel in the Hunter Creek study area (Oregon Department of Transportation, 2010):

- Hunter Creek Road bridge, RKM 9.1

- Hunter Creek Road bridge, RKM 3.5

- Hunter Creek Road bridge, RKM 0.6

- Highway 101 bridge, RKM 0

Our review of the bridge-inspection reports for these four sites focused primarily on comparing repeat channel cross-sections and secondarily on reviewing supplemental data such as underwater reports, photographs, and scour assessments, which also are helpful for assessing channel condition adjacent to these bridges.

Channel cross-section surveys were collected at three bridges in 1994, 2004, and 2008 (fig. 5A–C) and at the Highway 101 bridge near the mouth in 1998 and 2010 (fig. 5D). Repeat channel cross-sections taken near the Hunter Creek Road bridge at RKM 9.1 show that the elevation of the thalweg has remained similar over time even though the channel has shifted from bank to bank between surveys (fig. 5A). The thalweg near the Hunter Creek Road bridge at RKM 3.5 maintained a similar elevation while shifting its position and depositing nearly a meter of material along the left bank from 1994 to 2004, which was followed by 0.55 m of aggradation from 2004 to 2008 (fig. 5B).

Farther downstream, near the Hunter Creek Road bridge at RKM 0.6 (fig. 5C), the channel aggraded from 1994 to 2004, resulting in nearly 2 m of deposition along the left side of the channel and 0.84 m of deposition in the thalweg. From 2004 to 2008, however, the channel incised through this fill, resulting in a 2008 cross section that resembles the 1994 cross-section and little net change in elevation from 1994 to 2008 (fig. 5C). At Hunter Creek near the Highway 101 bridge, repeat surveys from 1998 and 2010 show that this cross-section has remained relatively stable with little net change (< 0.3 m) in bed elevation for much of the cross section (fig. 5D).

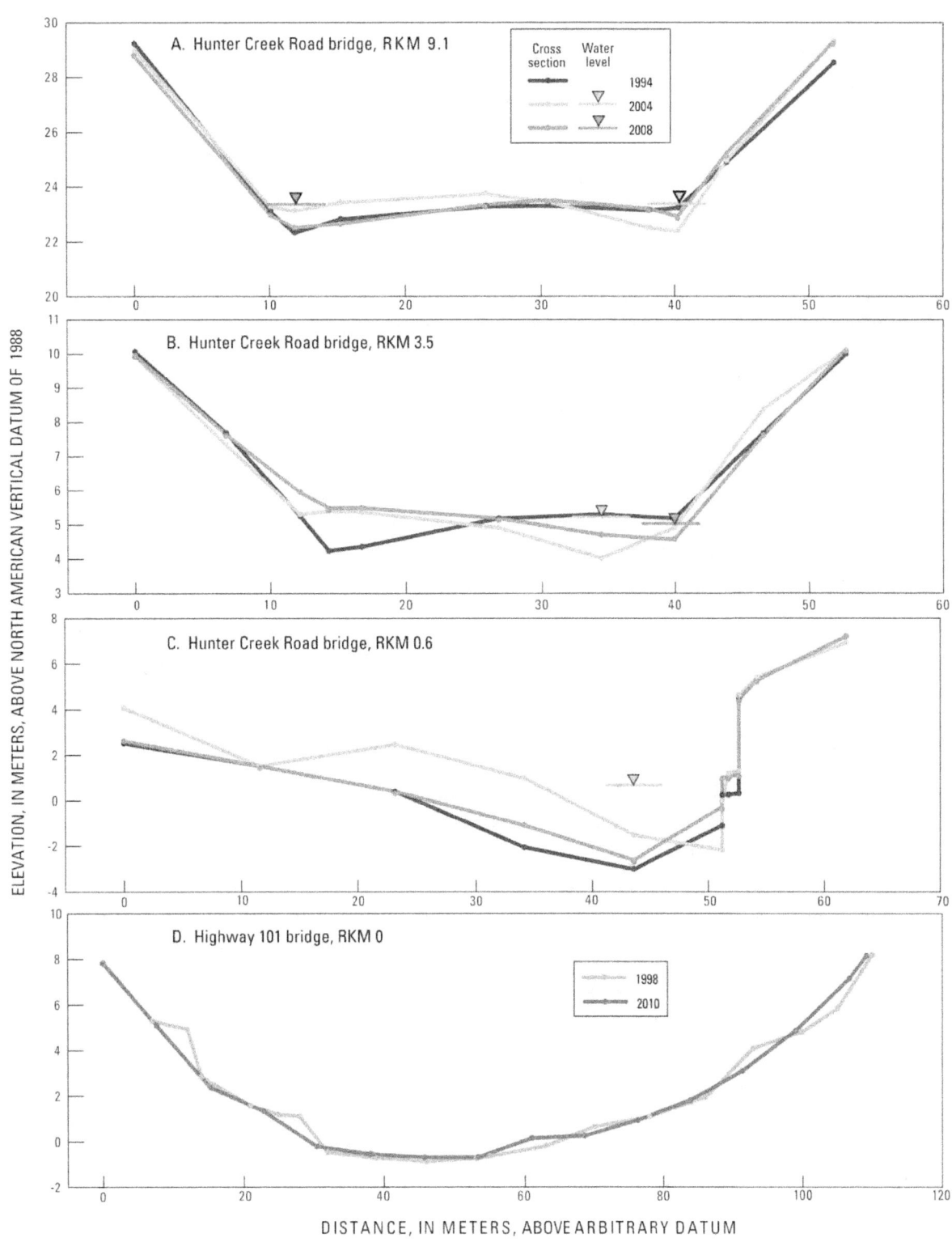

Figure 5. Repeat channel cross-sections collected by Oregon Department of Transportation at Hunter Creek Road crossings at (A) river kilometer (RKM) 9.1, (B) RKM 3.5, and (C) RKM 0.6, as well as (D) Highway 101 bridge crossing at RKM 0. Water elevation, where available, is indicated on the cross-sections over the thalweg. Cross-sections are shown looking downstream.

21

The bridge-inspection reports also state that the channel near all of the Hunter Creek Road bridges is prone to some level of bank slumping, and scour and erosion varies considerably from site to site. For example, the channel near the Highway 101 bridge is considered a low scour risk because of the influence of tide even though scour at the RKM 0.6 bridge led to undermining of the piers, resulting in an "unstable" rating. Combined, the bridge-inspection reports show that the channel at these bridge crossings is dynamic and subject to frequent channel shifting, aggradation, and incision. Despite this dynamism, the limited cross-section data reviewed in this study indicate that the channel near RKM 3.5 was the only location to experience substantial net change (+0.55 m in thalweg elevation) from 1994 to 2004. The channel at RKM 9.6 and 0 showed little net change in channel morphology or thalweg elevation between the first and last surveys, whereas the elevation of the thalweg at RKM 0.6 increased 0.84 m from 1994 to 2004, but did not exhibit substantial net change from 1994 to 2008.

Repeat Delineation of Gravel Bars, Channel Centerlines, and Channel Width, 1940–2009

Using the Geographic Information System (GIS) program ESRI ArcMap 9.3.1, we digitized gravel bars, channel centerlines, and wetted-channel edges throughout the study area from aerial photographs collected in 1940, 1965, 2005, and 2009 (table 4) to assess spatial and temporal trends in bar and channel features. Scanned black-and-white photographs from 1940 and 1965 were acquired from the University of Oregon Map Library and georeferenced using techniques similar to those in Wallick and others (2011). For mapping purposes, gravel bars were defined as exposed bed-material sediments greater than 200 m^2 in area and included both lateral and medial bars.

Although bars were not classified according to grain size, field observations made during July 2010 indicated that most bars, including those in the tidally affected portion of the Lower Study Reach, mainly were composed of gravel. Most of the mapped bars had little to no vegetation, but some bars had small areas that were partly or wholly covered by grasses, shrubs, and (to a lesser extent) mature trees.

The quality of underlying photographs and errors introduced by georeferencing and digitizing processes are three of many potential sources of uncertainty in digital channel maps (Gurnell, 1997; Mount and Louis, 2005; Hughes and others, 2006; Walter and Tullos, 2009). Aerial photographs of the Hunter Creek study area were of sufficient resolution (table 4) and generally free of glare and shadow, enabling precise mapping. The 1940 and 1965 photographs were georeferenced with a minimum of 15 ground-control points concentrated near the main channel and rectified with a second-order polynomial transformation. The total root mean square error (RMSE) values of the rectified photographs from 1940 and 1965 indicated that horizontal-position uncertainties associated with the georectification process ranged from 2.9 to 5.9 m, but averaged 5.8 m for the 1940 photographs and 3.7 m for the 1965 photographs. Since control points were concentrated near the channel, error associated with mapped features along channel corridor should be lower than the total RMSE values for the entire photograph. Delineation of bars, channel centerlines, and wetted-channel edges at a scale of 1:2,000 was verified by project team members to ensure consistent delineation of features among years and throughout the study area and consistency with the delineation protocol of Wallick and others (2011). Lastly, while streamflow on the dates of aerial-photograph acquisition is unknown, all aerial photographs used in this study were acquired during low-flow months (table 4), minimizing potential mapping error introduced by flow variations.

Results for Repeat Bar Delineation, 1940–2009

The total area of gravel bars delineated within the 12.4-km long study reach was 502,230 m^2 in 1940, 363,150 m^2 in 1965, and 236,100 m^2 in 2005 (table 6). From 2005 to 2009, total bar area remained relatively stable, increasing by 2 percent to 240,520 m^2. In 2009, unit bar area, or the total area of gravel bars per meter of channel (m^2/m), equates to 19.4 m^2/m. This value exceeds similar measurements for the bedrock-dominated Umpqua River, which drains an area nearly 41 times larger than Hunter Creek (unit bar area was 5–18 m^2/m for fluvial reaches on the Umpqua River; Wallick and others, 2011). For comparison, the gravel-rich Chetco River basin is about eight times the size of the Hunter Creek basin and had approximately 49.9 m^2 of gravel bars per meter of channel in 2005 within its 18.4-km long study area (Wallick and others, 2010).

Examination of the repeat delineation of gravel bars shows that the location, abundance, and size of gravel bars in Hunter Creek mainly dictated by valley physiography and the associated increase in valley width as the river approaches its mouth. Historically, smaller bars were located in confined segments such as the narrow canyon extending from RKM 6 to 8.4 (figs. 6A and 7). Conversely, the largest dynamic bars were located in wide areas of the floodplain including RKM 0–3 (figs. 6A and 8) in the Lower Study Reach and RKM 8.4–9 in the Upper Study Reach and are associated with channel shifting, bar growth, and erosion.

Table 6. Summary of changes in bar features and channel length, 1940–2009, for the Hunter Creek study area, southwestern Oregon.

[m², square meter; km, kilometer; m²/m, square meter per meter (bar area per meter of channel)]

	Entire study area				Lower Study Reach				Upper Study Reach			
	1940	1965	2005	2009	1940	1965	2005	2009	1940	1965	2005	2009
Total area of gravel bars (m²)	502,230	363,150	236,100	240,520	296,470	171,710	113,500	114,580	205,750	191,440	122,600	125,940
Unit bar area, normalized by 2009 centerline length (m²/m)	40.5	29.3	19.0	19.4	49.4	28.6	18.9	19.1	32.1	29.9	19.1	19.7
Percent net change in bar area, 1940–2009			-52				-61				-39	
Number of bars	71	70	96	82	29	32	43	41	42	38	53	41
Average gravel bar area (m²)	7,070	5,190	2,460	2,930	10,220	5,370	2,640	2,790	4,900	5,040	2,310	3,070
Maximum gravel bar area (m²)	52,610	36,010	32,050	19,090	52,610	28,790	32,050	19,090	39,640	36,010	15,980	15,900
Channel centerline length (km)	12.6	12.6	12.5	12.4	6.1	5.9	6.0	6.0	6.5	6.7	6.5	6.4
Percent net change in channel centerline length, 1940–2009			-1.3				-1.6				-1.1	

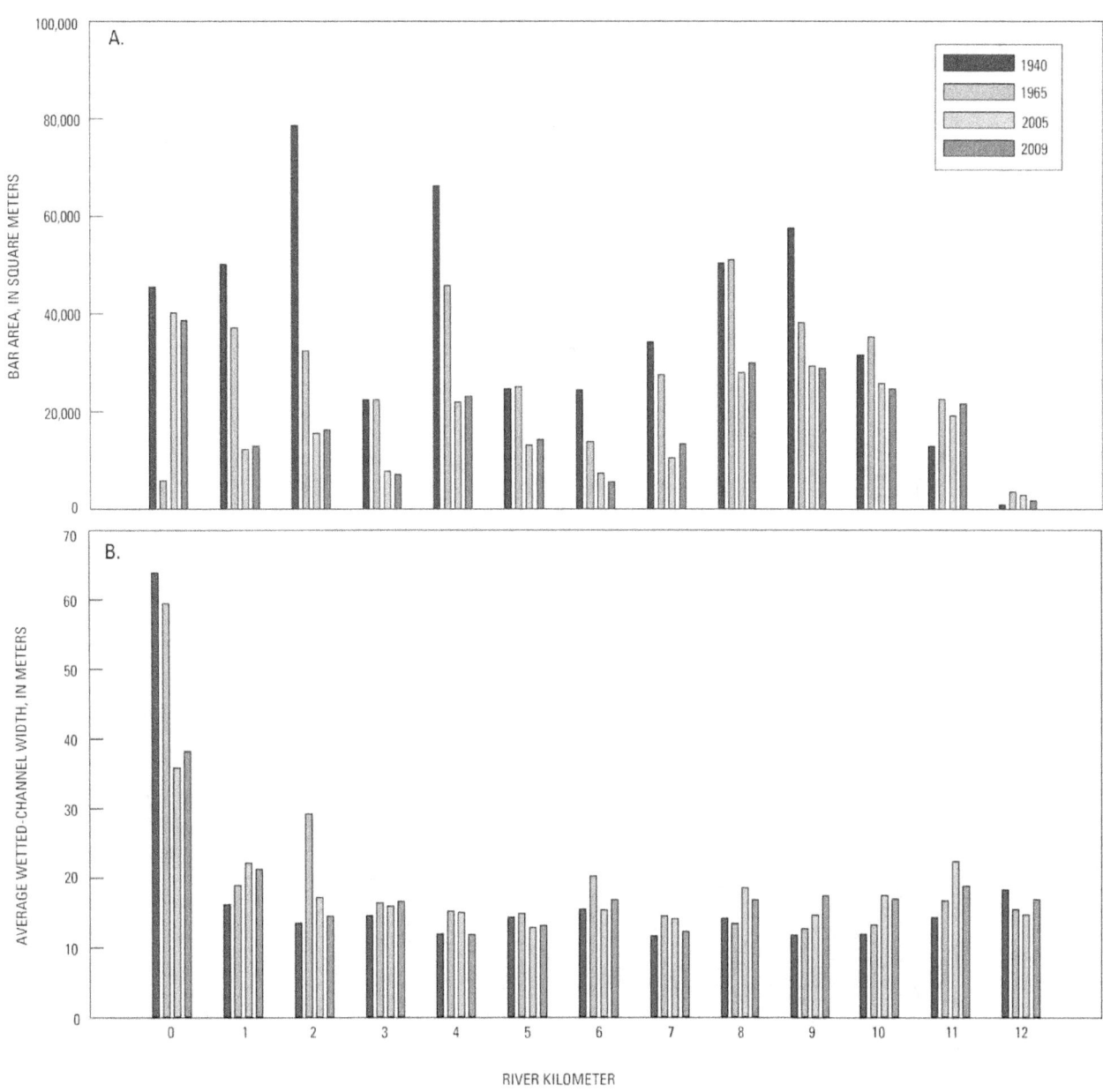

Figure 6. (A) Distribution and size of gravel-bar accumulations and (B) wetted-channel width by river kilometer transect as mapped from 1940, 1965, 2005, and 2009 aerial photographs for the Hunter Creek study area, southwestern Oregon. Note: The study area ended at river kilometer 12.4 and, thus, this transect includes data for only 0.4 kilometer.

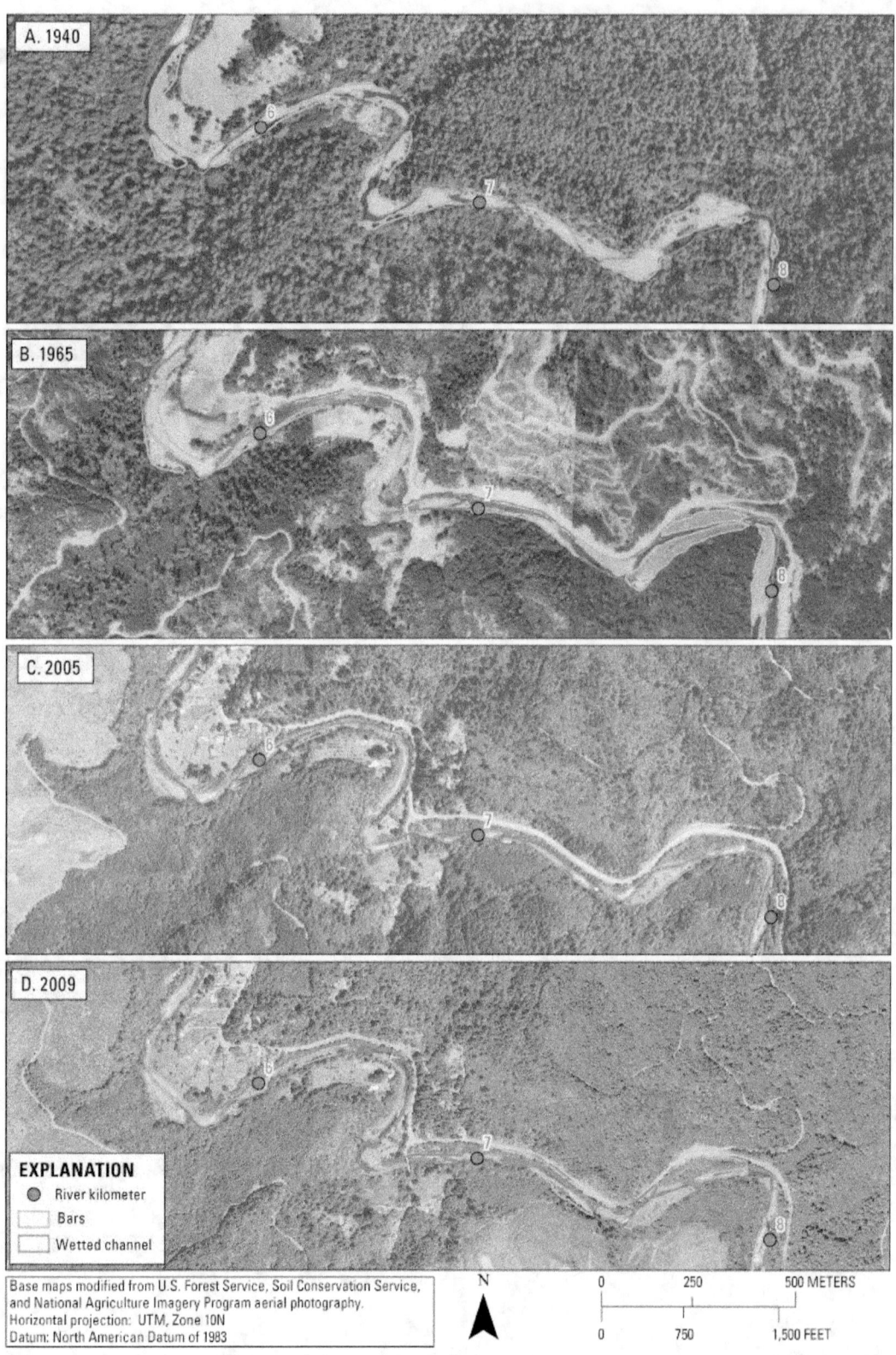

Figure 7. Examples of gravel bars and wetted channel edge as delineated from 1940, 1965, 2005, and 2009 aerial photographs for river-kilometer transects 6–8, where the active channel is confined in the Hunter Creek study area, southwestern Oregon.

26

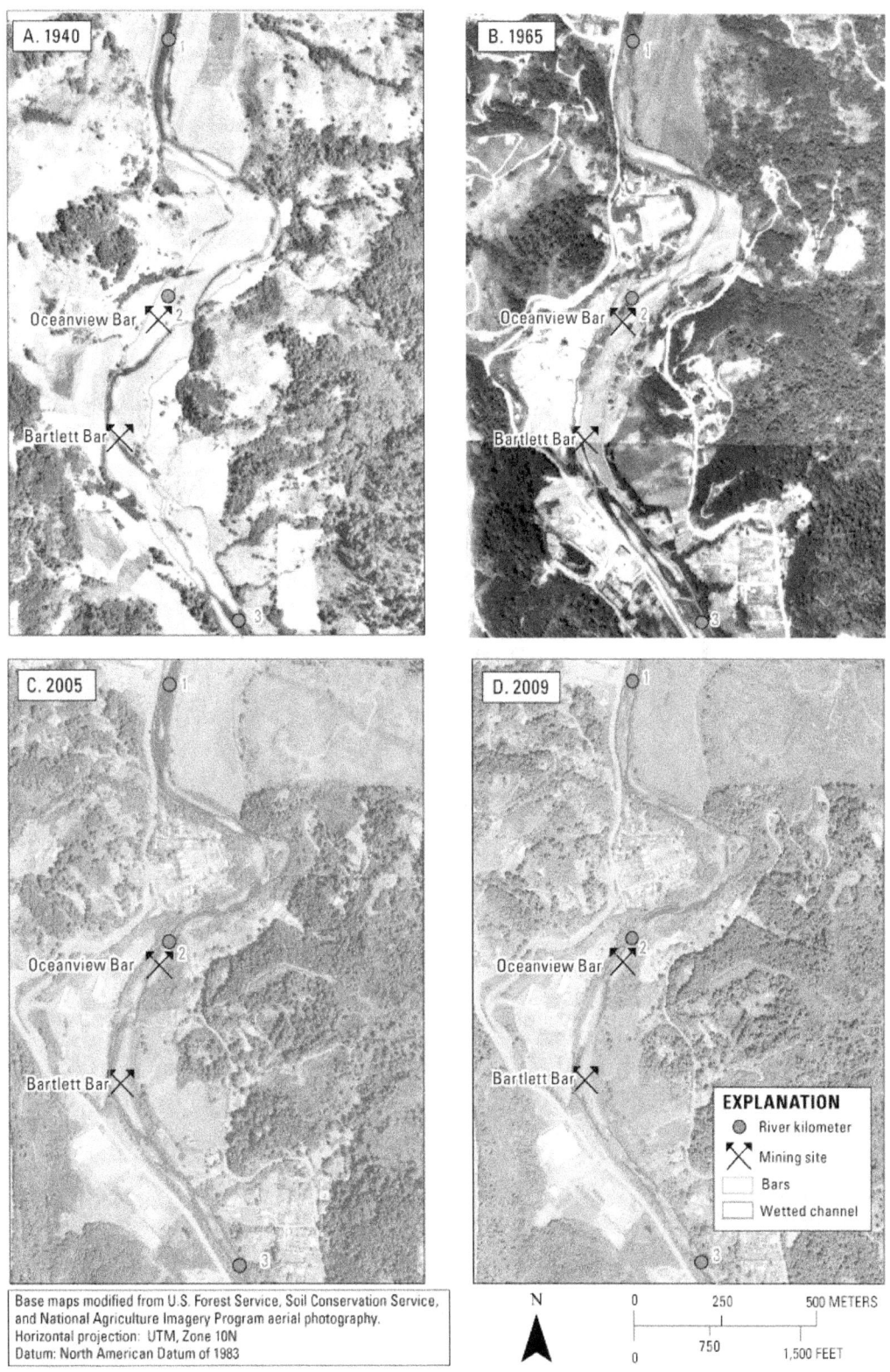

Figure 8. Examples of gravel bars and wetted channel edge as delineated from 1940, 1965, 2005, and 2009 aerial photographs for river kilometers 1–3, where the active channel is unconfined in the Hunter Creek study area, southwestern Oregon.

Throughout the Hunter Creek system, areal coverage of gravel bars has declined 52-percent since 1940 (fig. 9 and table 6). Bars near the mouth of Hunter Creek deviated from the overall systemwide decline, increasing substantially from 1965 to 2005, likely following captures of two floodplain pits and deposition and reworking of bed-material on river right (figs. 6A and 10). This increase in bar area near the mouth also may be affected by differences in tide levels at the time of aerial-photograph acquisition.

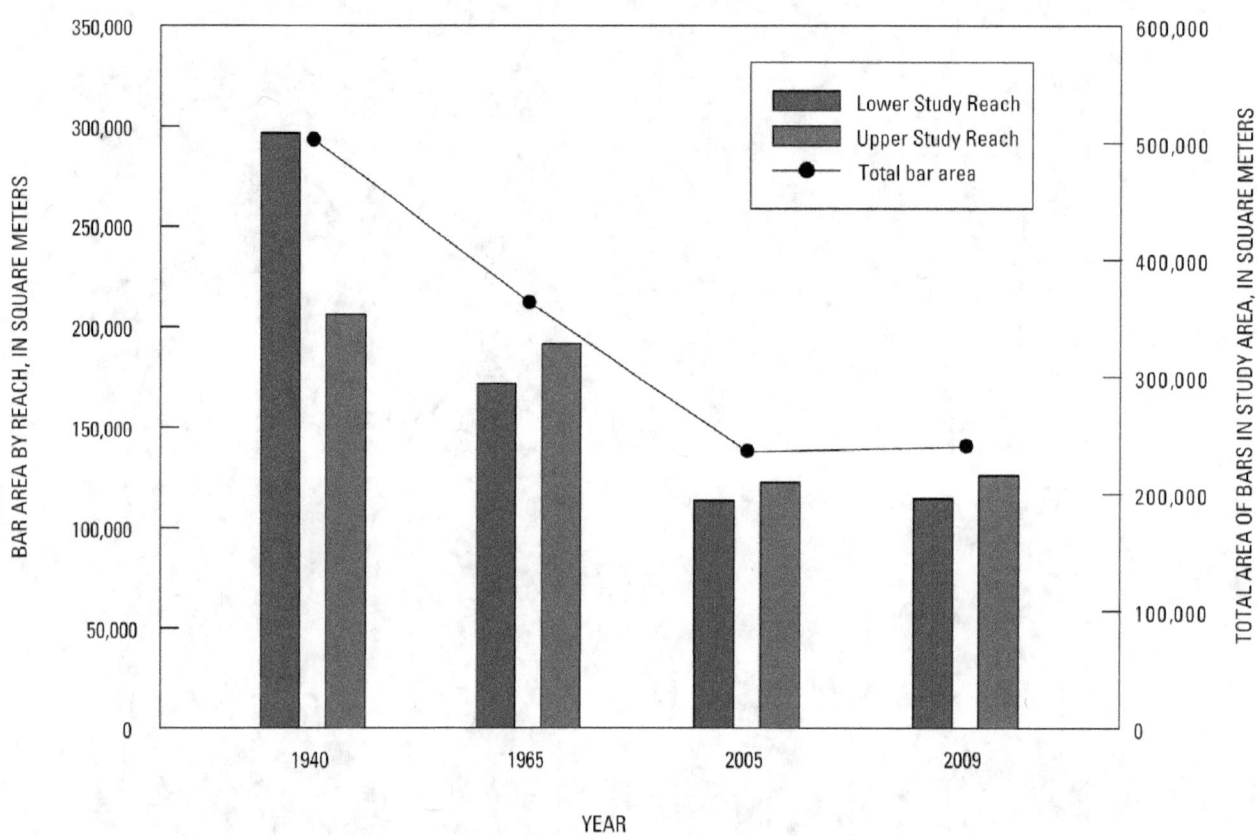

Figure 9. Gravel bar area for the two study reaches (denoted by bars) and study area (denoted by line) as delineated from aerial photographs dated 1940, 1965, 2005, and 2009 for Hunter Creek, southwestern Oregon,.

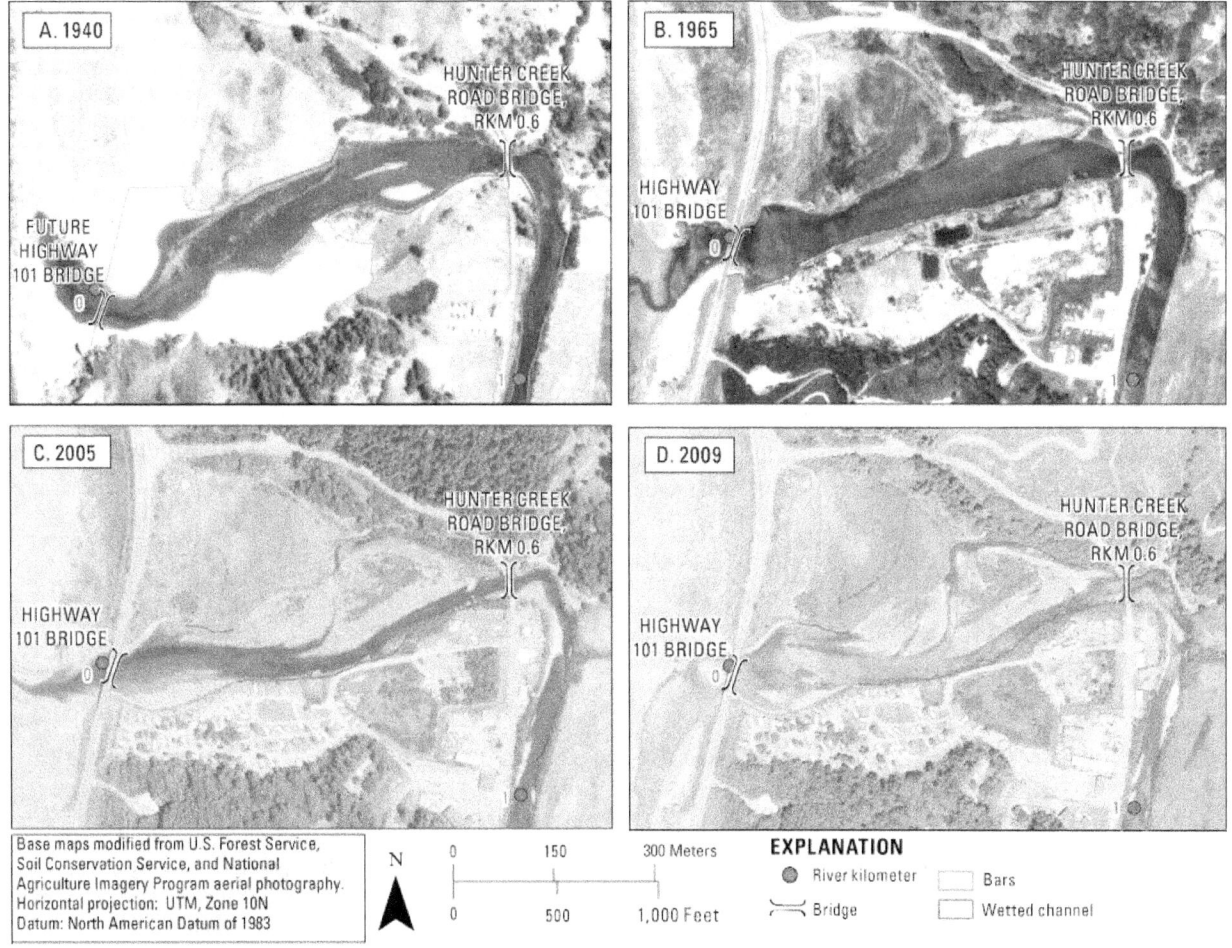

Figure 10. Gravel bars and wetted channel edge as delineated from 1940, 1965, 2005, and 2009 aerial photographs for the mouth of Hunter Creek, southwestern Oregon. The lower 2.2 kilometers of Hunter Creek are tidally influenced. Approximate bridge locations are denoted by river kilometer (RKM)

Although the total area of bars has decreased substantially since 1940, the number of bars has not changed systematically. Consequently, the loss of bar area mostly is the result of individual bars becoming smaller, with average bar size diminishing from 7,070 m^2 in 1940 to 2,930 m^2 in 2009 (table 6).

The apparent overall reduction in bar area along Hunter Creek may be partly owing to some challenges in delineating bar surfaces. In particular, distinguishing the boundary between bar surfaces and the floodplain in the aerial photographs collected in 1940 was difficult, possibly leading to some overestimation of bar area for

this year. Ambiguity in delineating the outer boundary of bars from the 1940 photographs, however, is not a factor in the large decline in bar area evident in the much clearer 1965 and 2005 photographs.

Changes in bar area primarily are associated with the conversion of bare-bar surfaces to vegetated or developed surfaces. Development on former bar surfaces resulted in local declines in bar area (fig. 10). However, the greatest source of bar loss occurred as bar surfaces that were bare in 1940 became increasingly vegetated, likely with grasses and shrubs, in 1965 and 2005.

Because we defined and delineated gravel bars as exposed bed-material sediment, increases in vegetation at the expense of bare bars resulted in a reduction in mapped bar surfaces. Although these relict bar surfaces may be stabilized with vegetation and are therefore not mapped as bars, the underlying substrate remains available for future erosion and transport during high-flow events. Vegetation establishment on bar surfaces was especially pronounced along the historically dynamic, gravel-rich areas from RKM 1 to 2 (fig. 8) and near RKM 4 and coincided with large local losses in bar area (fig. 6A). Vegetation encroachment was minimal in the confined, upper 1.4 km of the study area (fig. 7). Further analysis of the trends in active channel width and vegetation coverage by type may provide additional insight into the mechanisms driving bar loss along Hunter Creek.

Similar patterns of bar loss owing to vegetation encroachment have been documented in the nearby Chetco River (Wallick and others, 2010) and Umpqua River (Wallick and others, 2011). In both basins, vegetation establishment on upper bar surfaces mainly followed the December 1964 flood and was attributed primarily to declines in peak flows, which probably owe to long-term climate cycles. The Oregon Coast generally experienced cool, wet conditions from 1946 to1976, but the period since 1976 has been overall warmer and drier with intermittent, shorter periods of cool, wet years (George Taylor, Oregon Climate Service, written commun., 1999).

Results for Channel Planform and Width, 1940–2009

Comparison of channel centerline length over time reveals that channel length has decreased by 1.3-percent throughout the study area from 1940 to 2009 with both reaches losing a net 0.1 km of centerline length (table 6). Specific areas with substantial channel shifting include RKM 0–0.6, 1.6–2.6, and 3.8–4.8 (figs. 8 and 10).

Comparison of wetted-channel width over time indicates some subtle changes in width from 1940 to 2009 (fig. 6B) such as near the mouth of Hunter Creek. However, these results do not indicate systemwide or systematic changes in width and do not correspond directly with changes in bar area. This preliminary analysis of wetted-channel width does not indicate channel incision or aggradation. More detailed delineation of the active-channel width (instead of wetted-channel width, which can be influenced by small differences in streamflow or tide) may help better quantify possible changes in channel width throughout the study area.

Road encroachment and mining of gravel bars, two direct disturbances to the active channel of Hunter Creek, have had no clear effect on channel planform. Hunter Creek Road, constructed in the 1940s, impinges in several places upon the historical active channel (fig. 3). The road alignment, however, does not appear to have had a substantial effect on subsequent channel change (fig. 11). The three Hunter Creek Road bridge crossings were constructed at confined, stable segments that do not show major planform changes from 1940 to 2009 (for example, the Hunter Creek bridge crossing near RKM 3.5 shows only minor changes in bar area, fig. 11).

Hunter Creek Road was constructed on three surfaces mapped as bars in 1940 (such as RKM 4.5, 7.6, and 9.6). In all instances, however, reachwide vegetation encroachment and localized development appear to have had larger impacts on local bar loss than road building (as illustrated for RKM 4.5, fig. 11). This assessment, however, does not take into account possible fill activities associated with road construction and subsequent protection. Additionally, road crossings throughout the river basin may increase erosion and fine sediment inputs that can cause subtle changes in pool morphology. Such possible changes in the transport and deposition of fine sediment were not addressed by this study.

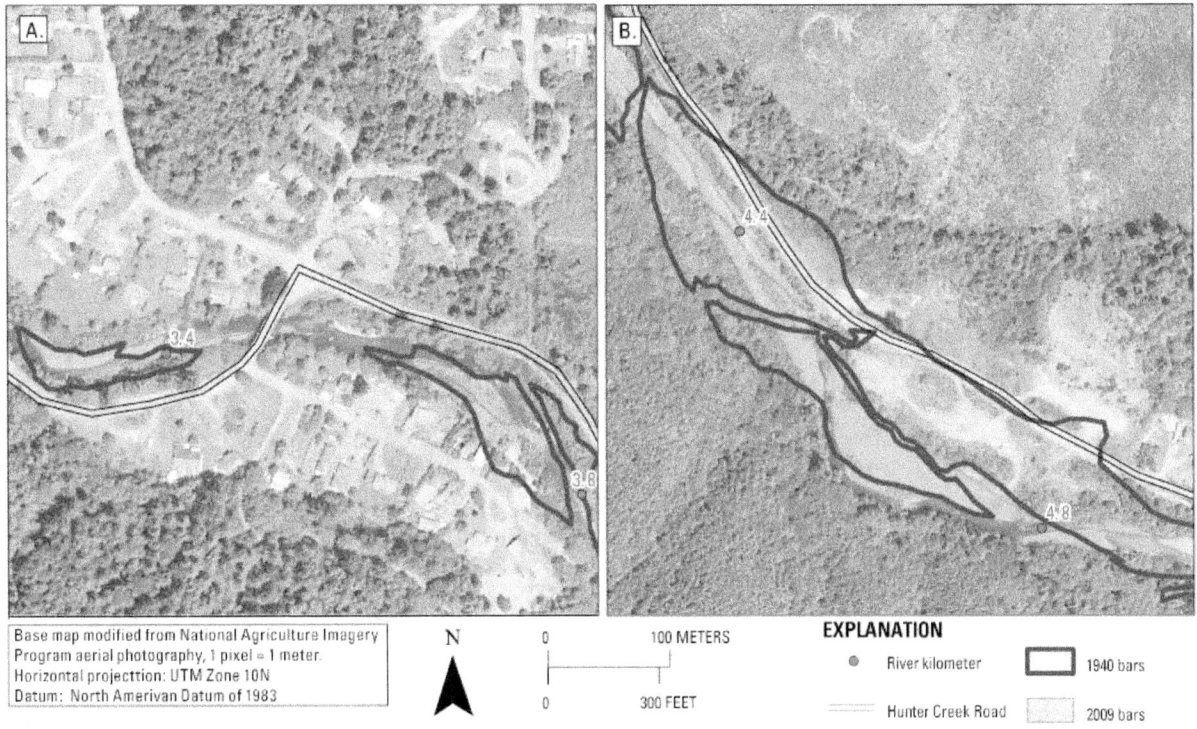

Base map modified from National Agriculture Imagery
Program aerial photography, 1 pixel = 1 meter.
Horizontal projecttion: UTM Zone 10N
Datum: North Amerivan Datum of 1983

N

0   100 METERS

0   300 FEET

EXPLANATION

● River kilometer   ☐ 1940 bars

Hunter Creek Road   2009 bars

Figure 11. Examples of gravel bars and wetted channel edge as delineated from 1940, 1965, 2005, and 2009 aerial photographs for sections where the Hunter Creek Road has impinged on the historical active channel in the Hunter Creek study area, southwestern Oregon.

At the three active in-channel gravel-extraction sites, the position of the channel has been nearly stable since the 1965 photographs (fig. 12, next page). Although bar area has decreased from 1940 to 2009 at the three extraction sites, these declines are consistent with reductions throughout the study area and are not obviously attributable to local gravel extraction. Future analyses of temporal changes in channel width, sinuosity, and bar morphology based on aerial photographs and LiDAR would be useful in discerning whether mined sites have been specifically affected.

Bed-Material Particle-Size Analyses

During the July 2010 reconnaissance trip, we measured surface particle-size distributions and collected subsurface bulk samples at two actively mined gravel bars in the study area: Menasha Bar (RKM 4.1) in the Lower Study Reach and Conn Creek Bar (RKM 9.7) in the

Upper Study Reach (fig. 12). Samples were collected prior to the annual mining of these sites. At each site, the diameter of 200 surface particles was measured using a modified grid technique (Kondolf and others, 2003) such that measurements were taken at 0.3-m increments along two parallel 30-m tapes (fig. 13A–D). The tapes were spaced 1–2 m apart and were aligned parallel to the long axis of the bar. Clast-diameter measurements were made using an aluminum template (Federal Interagency Sediment Project US–SAH-97 Gravelometer) that enables standardized measurement of sediment clasts greater than 2 mm in diameter. Bulk samples of subsurface material were collected at the same locations as the surface-measurement sites by removing approximately 0.5 to1 m^2 of bar-surface material and then collecting 65–78 kg of bar-substrate material. The bulk samples then were dried and analyzed for ½-phi particle sizes by the U.S. Geological Survey Sediment Laboratory in Vancouver, Washington.

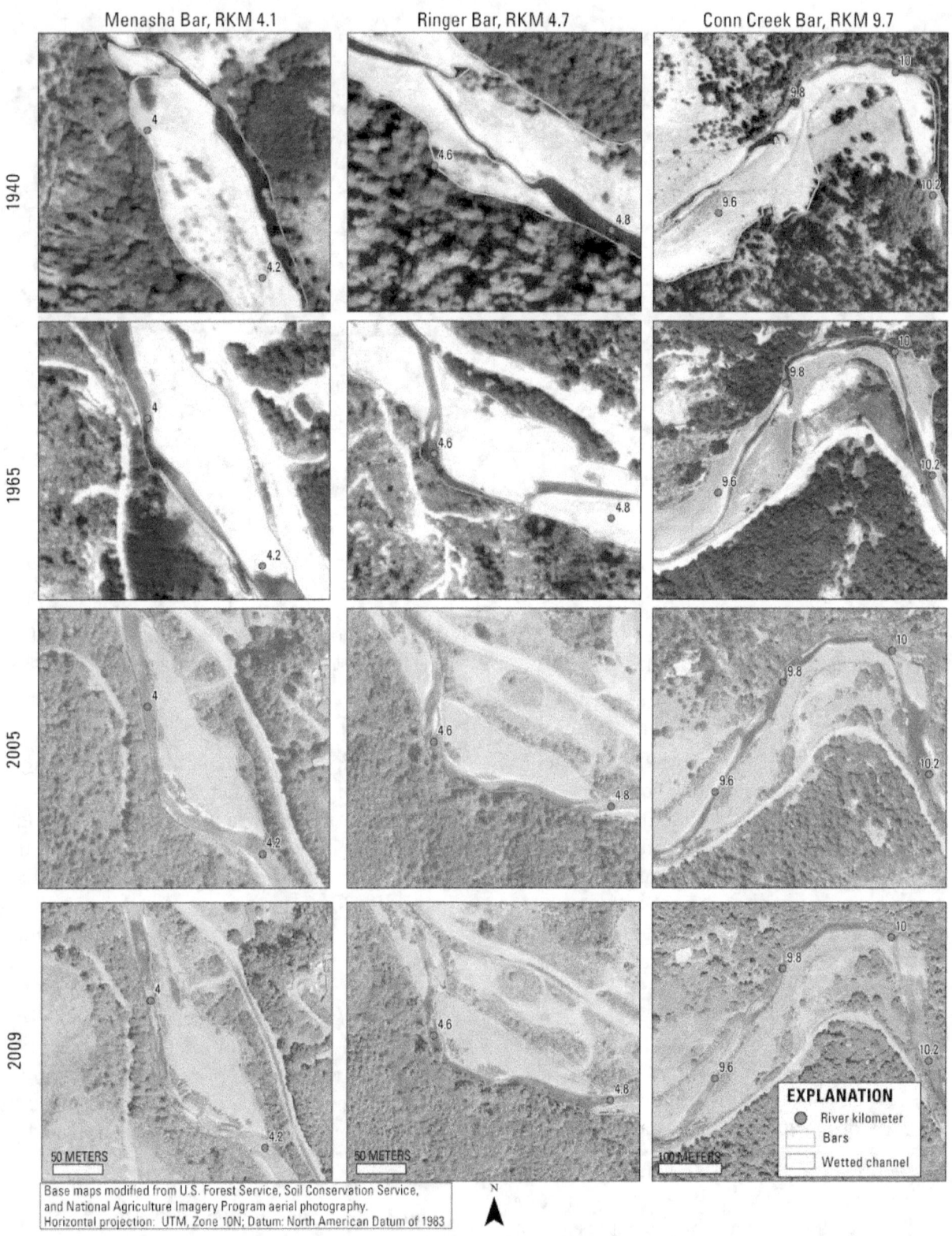

Figure 12. Gravel bars and wetted channel edge as delineated from 1940, 1965, 2005, and 2009 aerial photographs for Menasha Bar (river kilometer [RKM] 4.1), Ringer Bar (RKM 4.7), and Conn Creek Bar (RKM 9.7) along Hunter Creek, southwestern Oregon.

Figure 13. Bed-material-sampling sites at Conn Creek (A–B) and Menasha (C–D) Bars along Hunter Creek, southwestern Oregon.

Bar-surface material was approximately equal in size to bar-subsurface material at Conn Creek Bar, whereas it was distinctly coarser than the bar-subsurface material at Menasha Bar (fig. 14A–B). A relatively coarse surface layer (or armoring) is typical for gravel-bed rivers and can be the result of selective scouring of fine sediments or selective deposition of larger particle clasts (Bunte and Abt, 2001). Calculating the armoring ratio, or the ratio of the median grain sizes (D_{50}) of the surface to subsurface layers, provides an indication of the degree of armoring. This ratio typically is close to 1 for rivers with a high sediment supply and approaches or exceeds 2 for supply-limited rivers (Bunte and Abt, 2001). The calculated armoring ratios were 0.97 and 1.5 at Conn Creek and Menasha Bars, respectively, which are consistent with high bed-material transport rates (fig. 14A–B). For comparison, most armoring ratios reported for the Chetco and Umpqua Rivers exceeded 1.5 (Wallick and others, 2010; 2011). Because bar texture can vary greatly between sites on gravel-bed rivers (Wilcock and others, 2009), analyses including additional sampling at sites without recent gravel mining or recreational disturbance would refine assessments of transport and sediment-supply conditions and longitudinal trends in bed-material (fig. 14C).

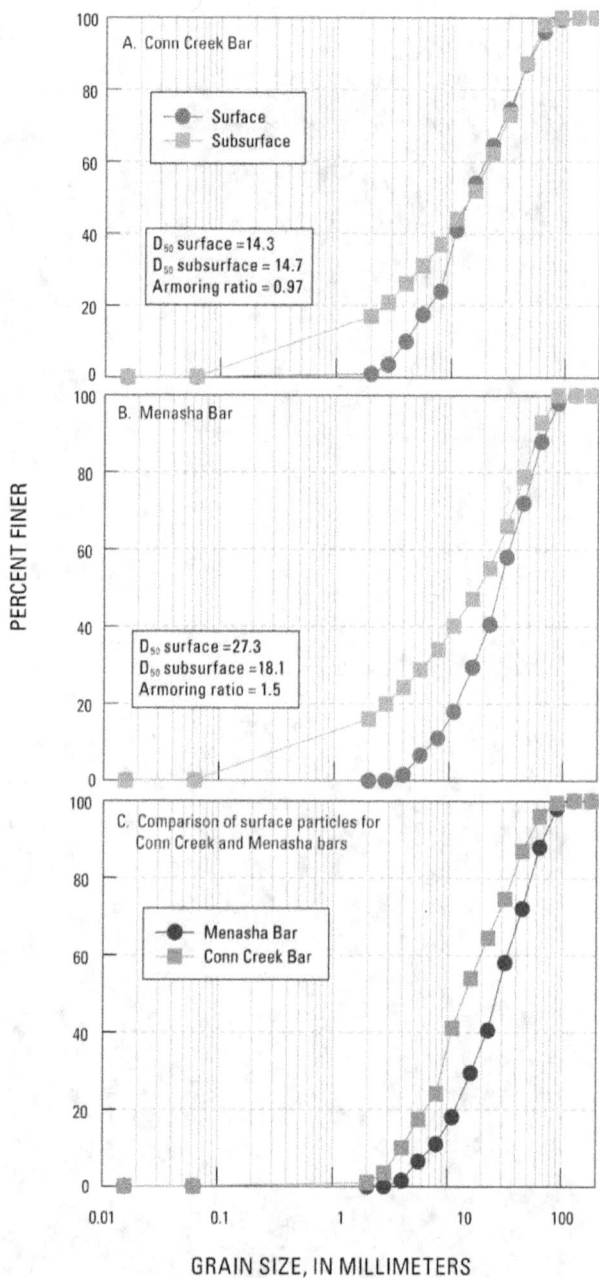

Figure 14. Size distributions of surface and subsurface particles collected in July 2010 at two sites along Hunter Creek, southwestern Oregon. Surface-particle-size distributions were sampled by a count of 200 clasts; subsurface distributions were sampled from bulk sample below the armor layer. (A) particle data for the Conn Creek Bar, (B) particle data for the Menasha Bar, and (C) comparison of bar-surface particle sizes at the two bars. D_{50} is the measured median particle size in millimeters.

Summary of Findings

On the basis of field observations, delineation of bar and channel features from aerial photographs, and review of existing datasets and studies, the lower 12.4 km of the Hunter Creek study area is logically divided into two study reaches: (1) the Upper Study Reach, where the relatively narrow channel is confined by a bedrock canyon in its upper 1.4 km and then fully alluvial in its lower 5 km with smaller bars, and (2) the Lower Study Reach, where the channel is completely alluvial, generally wider, and more dynamic and has larger bars. Both reaches contain locally confined and unconfined segments as well as gravel bars used for historical and ongoing aggregate extraction.

Table 7 contains a summary of project findings by dataset and reach. Repeat delineation of gravel bars shows that bar area throughout the study area declined 52 percent from 1940 to 2009 (table 6). Bar loss was greatest in the lower 6 km of Hunter Creek (table 6, fig. 9, and table 7).

Some of the apparent loss in bar area possibly owes to mapping uncertainties; however, our preliminary assessment is that encroachment of vegetation onto the upper bar surfaces and subsequent stabilization of these formerly active surfaces likely caused this bar loss (such as shown in fig. 8). Vegetation encroachment and associated declines in bar area possibly were associated with long-term reductions in peak flows as noted for the Chetco and Umpqua Rivers (Wallick and others, 2010; 2011). During the December 1964 flood, the Chetco and Umpqua Rivers experienced extensive vegetation removal and sediment deposition on upper bar surfaces, leading to substantial increases in bar area on both rivers (Wallick and others, 2010; 2011). Because Hunter Creek experienced a 28-percent loss in bar area from 1940 to 1965 (table 6), indicating a muted response to this flood event, further investigation of peak-flow patterns in the basin would be helpful for understanding channel and bed-material responses to peak-flows over time.

Table 7. Summary of findings for the Hunter Creek study area, southwestern Oregon

[RKM, river kilometer; km, kilometer; NA, not applicable; D_{50}, median grain diameter; mm, millimeter]

Dataset	Lower Study Reach (RKM 0–6)	Upper Study Reach (RKM 6–12.4)
Review of previous studies	Incision, bank instability, and loss of point bars and pools noted in lower 3.9 km (EA Engineering, Science, and Technology, 1998).	NA
Qualitative review of pre and post extraction surveys, 2006–10	Surveys tentatively indicate that the Menasha and Ringer Bars sites are: (1) dynamic with annual deposition and erosion, and (2) re-built by deposition post-mining to approximately pre-mining elevations.	NA
Comparison of repeat cross-section surveys collected at bridge crossings, 1994–2010	The channel at RKM 3.5 shifted between 1994 and 2004, then aggraded 0.55 m in thalweg elevation between 2004 and 2008. Otherwise, the channel at RKM 0 and 0.6 had little net change between surveys.	The channel at RKM 9.1 shifted position between 1994 and 2004, but was otherwise stable with no substantial changes in thalweg elevation.
Repeat mapping of bar area and centerline length, 1940–2009	Bar area decreased 61 percent from 1940 to 2009. This loss was greatest in RKM 0–4. Centerline length decreased 0.1 km from 1940 to 2009.	Bar area decreased 39 percent from 1940 to 2009. This loss was greatest in RKM 7–9. Centerline length decreased 0.1 km from 1940 to 2009.
Particle size data collected in July 2010	At Menasha Bar, surface D_{50} = 27.3 mm, subsurface D_{50} = 18.1 mm; Armoring ratio = 1.5.	At Conn Creek Bar, surface D_{50} = 14.3 mm, subsurface D_{50} = 14.7 mm; Armoring ratio = 0.97.

Table 7. Summary of findings for the Hunter Creek study area, southwestern Oregon—continued.

[RKM, river kilometer; km, kilometer; NA, not applicable; D_{50}, median grain diameter; mm, millimeter]

Dataset	Lower Study Reach (RKM 0–6)	Upper Study Reach (RKM 6–12.4)
Summary	Dynamic alluvial channel has capacity for both lateral and vertical adjustments in channel position. Large declines in bar area tentatively correspond with slight loss in centerline length. Repeat cross-section surveys and field observations do not indicate obvious recent incision. Additional analyses are needed to determine cause of bar loss and verify incision noted by previous study.	Uppermost 1.4 km of channel stable with little likelihood of long-term incision due to confinement by bedrock canyon. Between RKM 6 and 11, the channel is predominantly alluvial and subject to channel shifting, bar growth, and erosion. Although bar area has declined substantially between 1940 and 2009, repeat surveys and armoring ratio indicate tentative balance between sediment supply and transport capacity.

Additionally, reductions in bar area also may have been affected by incision (EA Engineering, Science, and Technology, 1998). Reconnaissance-level field observations, an analysis of wetted-width changes, and repeat channel cross-sections reviewed in this study, however, do not indicate substantial bed lowering. Channel length throughout the study area remained relatively stable, declining 0.1 km in both reaches, over the 69-year analysis period. Areas with substantial channel shifting and decreased sinuosity do coincide with areas of substantial bar loss (for example RKM 1.4–2.8 and 4.2–4.8). Although such findings may be indicative of local incision, they also may reflect that the Hunter Creek channel is dynamic and subject to lateral channel shifting, bar growth, and erosion.

Particle-size measurements from two actively mined sites broadly support the findings from the repeat bar mapping and cross-section surveys. Armoring ratios at Conn Creek Bar (RKM 9.7) and Menasha Bar (RKM 4.1) were 0.97 and 1.5, respectively, indicating that sediment supply is approximately balanced by transport capacity.

In summary, although Hunter Creek is tidally affected in its lowermost 2.2 km, gravel bars extend to the frequently shifting mouth of the river (fig. 10), indicating substantial gravel transport through the reach and to the Pacific Ocean. Gravel transport and deposition evidently have kept pace with Holocene sea-level rise, filling the incised valley and creating a graded-river profile to the sea and the lack of a fluvial estuary. These aspects of river and valley character, in conjunction with the nearly continuous alluvial channel in the lower 11 km and presence of bars to the mouth of the river, are strong evidence that bed-material transport to and through the Hunter Creek study area is —transport-limited" in the sense that bed-material transport depends on flow and bed-material characteristics rather than on bed-material supplied to the study area. In this respect, Hunter Creek is more similar to the Chetco River (Wallick and others, 2010) than the supply-limited Umpqua River (Wallick and others, 2011).

Outstanding Issues and Possible Approaches

This reconnaissance-level analysis provides a framework and baseline information for understanding bed-material transport in the Hunter Creek basin. Future efforts addressing several data gaps and issues as well as key analyses (as outlined below) could greatly refine the understanding of historical and ongoing bed-material transport processes and their effects on channel morphology. Additionally, addressing and understanding these data gaps would provide a solid basis for evaluating future hydrologic and geomorphic changes in the Hunter Creek system.

Hunter Creek Streamflow

Modeling and predicting bed-material transport require high-quality streamflow information, particularly for peak flows. As of 2011, no streamflow-gaging station is operated routinely in the lower Hunter Creek basin. Although this study used regional-regression equations to estimate discharge for a range of flood events, these estimates include considerable uncertainty (table 2). For predicting bed-material transport within the study reach, such a gaging station optimally would be located near the upstream boundary of the study area such as the Hunter Creek Road bridge crossing at RKM 9.1 downstream of the confluence of Conn and Hunter Creeks. Additionally, repeat measurements of stage and discharge (obtained by USGS technicians during routine maintenance of the gage) form the basis of a specific gage analysis and could be used to track local changes in bed elevation over time following the approach used on the Chetco and Umpqua Rivers by Wallick and others (2010; 2011).

Bed-Material Transport Rates and Sediment Budget

Understanding possible effects of instream gravel extraction on channel condition and longitudinal and temporal changes in bed-material requires a thorough accounting of sediment inputs from upstream and lateral sources as well as sediment losses owing to particle attrition, transport, and storage. Such information would support a comparison of the volumes of gravel extracted from the system by ongoing mining activities relative to gravel delivered to the study area. An approach for expediently developing this sediment budget might include the following components:

1. Estimate sediment flux based upon equations of bedload transport. This approach will require installation of a streamflow-gaging station (as described above) and subsequent calculations of bedload transport using methods similar to those used on the Chetco River by Wallick and others (2010). A hydraulic model would enable more accurate estimations of energy slope (a critical component to the transport calculations), and facilitate transport capacity estimates for sites throughout the study area. Because Hunter Creek is mainly a single-thread channel, a one-dimensional model as developed for the Chetco River (Wallick and others, 2010) would probably be sufficient for estimating bed-material flux at the reach scale.

2. Collect direct measurements of bed-load transport in order to verify equations for bed-load transport and estimate actual bed-load fluxes. If possible, such measurements would be collected at a site of continuous-discharge measurement. The Hunter Creek Road bridges at RKM 9.1 and 3.5 are possible locations for high-quality bed-load measurements.

3. Estimate sediment flux based on mapped changes in bar area between two time periods, in a manner similar to the morphological approach used on the Chetco River by Wallick and others (2010). Ideally, this approach would use LiDAR data from two periods to directly calculate volumetric change in sediment storage. This method, however, also can be implemented using sequential aerial photographs along with a single LiDAR survey, such as the survey available for much of the Hunter Creek study area (table 4). Despite the inherent uncertainties associated with this type of analysis (Wallick and others, 2010), such data and analyses can support efficient monitoring of long-term changes in channel and floodplain conditions.

4. Review of pre- and post-gravel-extraction surveys. In-depth and comprehensive review of all mining surveys on Hunter Creek may provide insight into estimates

of coarse-gravel recruitment. While these surveys are subject to uncertainties and limitations and may be missing for some years and locations, all available data on gravel replenishment would help reduce uncertainty in sediment-flux estimates at extraction sites.

5. Assess bed-material composition throughout the study area. Additional observations of particle sizes would be required for calculating bed-material transport and also may support assessments of temporal changes in bed-material composition in conjunction with other study components.

Detailed Channel-Morphology Assessment

In this study, we delineated bar surfaces from aerial photographs taken in four different years, spanning 1940–2009, and found that bar area throughout the study area declined by 52-percent from 1940 to 2009 (table 6). This mapping could serve as the starting point for more detailed and comprehensive temporal analyses of morphological trends in Hunter Creek. In particular, possible drivers of the reduction in bar area include (1) vegetation encroachment onto previously active bar surfaces, (2) long-term decreases in peak flows, (3) lowering of the channel bed, and (4) other causes. To address each of these issues and better explain the large net decrease in bar area for Hunter Creek would require a comprehensive approach, drawing upon the following elements:

1. Detailed mapping of land cover for the lower 12.4 km of the Hunter Creek floodplain and for multiple time periods. This effort would involve delineating the active floodplain or floodplain features based on vegetation density, which may eliminate problems associated with determining the bar–floodplain boundary. Examining temporal changes in bare and vegetated surfaces would allow a more quantitative assessment of erosion, depo-

sition, and vegetation colonization during different periods and enable a more complete description of the processes driving bar evolution. Assessment of overall bar condition and evolution would benefit from supplemental bar delineations from aerial photographs collected in the early 1960s, 1970s, and 1990s.

2. Detailed mapping of channel features immediately before and after major floods to assess channel response to different magnitude floods and, ultimately, sediment flux and channel evolution in Hunter Creek. Possible floods for focusing this effort include the events of December 1964, November 1996, and January 1997. This effort optimally would be conducted in tandem with the construction a flood history for the basin.

3. Assessment of the potential relationship between vegetation encroachment and peak flows. In the Umpqua and Chetco River basins, historical declines in bar area are associated with long-term decreases in flood magnitude (Wallick and others, 2010; 2011). Determining whether a similar process of vegetation encroachment owing to decreasing peak flows is responsible for bar loss in the Hunter Creek basin would require estimation of historical-flood discharges, as described above. Additionally, determining the linkages between peak flows in Hunter Creek and climate factors related to flood peaks, such as the Pacific Decadal Oscillation, could support inferences of likely future changes in vegetation and overall channel conditions.

4. Investigation of planform changes and possible bed-level lowering. Although the preliminary analyses and datasets reviewed in this study do not indicate substantial incision along Hunter Creek, further investigations of planform evolution and bed-level lowering are warranted to determine whether local incision, par-

ticularly in the lower 3.9 km of Hunter Creek, has contributed to reachwide decreases in bar area. Since historical longitudinal surveys of the channel are unavailable, additional assessments of incision would rely upon detailed mapping of the active-channel features from different time periods and analysis of changes in channel width and sinuosity. Additional sources of data that may help to assess bed-level lowering include interviews with local landowners and a detailed assessment of bank stratigraphy in the lower 3.9 km.

5. More detailed review of the data available for bridges. A review of the as-built surveys and construction plans for publicly owned bridges on Hunter Creek may yield the data necessary to assess sediment thickness and changes in bed elevation. Construction plans, permits, and investigations of bridges owned by Curry County and private landowners also may yield useful information.

6. More detailed mapping and assessment of vegetation along the Hunter Creek corridor to assess (a) possible changes in the types of vegetation (such as invasive or water-tolerant species) present on bar surfaces over time and (b) broader linkages between riparian ecology, bar evolution, and flood histories.

7. Assess historical land-use activities, including timber-harvest practices, road building, and placer mining that may have contributed to changes in channel morphology and sediment-transport processes. Such information may be found through interviews with local landowners and historical documents available from historical societies, museums, and government records.

Legacy and Ongoing Effects of Land-Use Activities

Anthropogenic activities such as logging, in-stream gravel mining, and road placement likely affect sediment transport and deposition dynamics in Hunter Creek to varying degrees over time and throughout the river network. Quantitatively assessing the role of these factors on sediment dynamics would be challenging owing to likely interactions among these factors as well as their interactions with background and physical controls on sediment dynamics, such as basin topography, channel slope, geology, and hydrology. Yet, such an assessment would provide insight into sediment dynamics and may be more feasible in the Hunter Creek basin than other coastal basins.

Geomorphic and hydrologic processes often are altered by dredging, fire, flow regulations and dams, and substantial placer and hydraulic mining in coastal Oregon rivers such as the Chetco, Umpqua, and Rogue, but to a lesser extent in Hunter Creek. The preliminary morphological assessment presented in this report shows that the gravel bars are present throughout the study area and to the mouth of the river. Further investigations of fine- and coarse-sediment inputs associated with land-use activities may provide information on the relative fluxes of different clast sizes delivered to the study area and on an annual basis. An approach for investigating the relative importance of past activities on overall sediment dynamics would be to:

1. Determine the distribution of areas of active gravel transport and deposition and analyze temporal trends in channel and floodplain morphology with respect to land-use disturbances.

2. Assess changes in bar area and channel planform near historical gravel-extraction sites; Pratt (2004) reported a total of eight instream extraction sites along Hunter Creek in 1972.

3. Determine the relative contributions of fine and coarse sediments to the study area and identify storage and transport reaches and associated areas where fine sediments may fill in pool features.

Acknowledgments

The framework for this study was established with the guidance of Judy Linton of the Portland District of the U.S. Army Corps of Engineers. The project was administered by Judy Linton along with Bill Ryan and Pamela Konstant of the Oregon Department of State Lands. Tana Haluska, USGS Oregon Water Science Center, contributed to topographic analyses. Field assistance was provided by Xavier Rodriguez Lloveras, National Museum of Natural Science, Spanish National Research Council, Spain. Information on past gravel mining and detailed topographic surveys of mining sites was graciously provided by Dan Crumley of the Curry County Road Department. Access to Conn Creek Bar was courteously provided by Thomas Leith. Copies of Maguire (2001), EA Science, Technology, and Engineering (1998), and Pratt (2004) were graciously provided by Pam Blake, Oregon Department of Environmental Quality, Cindy Myers, South Coast and Lower Rogue Watershed Councils, and Jodi Fritts, Curry County Department of Public Services, respectively. Scanned copies of the 1940 and 1965 aerial photographs and a summary of available photographs were provided by University of Oregon Map Library personnel. Two colleagues provided insightful comments that improved this report.

References Cited

Atwood, Kay, 2008, Chaining Oregon—Surveying the public lands of the Pacific Northwest, 1851–1855: Granville, Ohio, The McDonald and Woodward Publishing Company, 267 p.

Beckham, S.D., 1986, Land of the Umpqua, a history of Douglas County, Oregon: Roseburg, Oregon, Douglas County Commissioners, 285 p.

Bunte, Kristin, and Abt, S.R., 2001, Sampling surface and subsurface particle-size distributions in wadeable gravel- and cobble-bed streams for analyses in sediment transport, hydraulics, and streambed monitoring: Fort Collins, Colorado, USDA Forest Service, Rocky Mountain Research Station, General Technical Report RMRS-GTR-74, 428 p.

Church, Michael, 1983, Pattern of instability in a wandering gravel bed channel, in Collinson, J.D., and Lewis, J., eds., Modern and ancient fluvial systems: International Association of Sedimentologists Special Publication 6, p. 169–180.

Church, Michael, 1988, Floods in cold climates, in Baker, V.R., Kochel, R.C., and Patton, P.C., eds., Flood geomorphology: New York, Wiley, p. 205–229.

Cooper, R.M., 2005, Estimation of peak discharges for rural, unregulated streams in Western Oregon: U.S. Geological Survey Scientific Investigations Report 2005–5116, 134 p.

EA Engineering, Science, and Technology, 1998, Hunter Creek watershed analysis—Prepared for the U.S. Department of Agriculture, U.S. Forest Service, Siskiyou National Forest: Hunt Valley Maryland, 114 p.

Farnell, J.E., 1981, Curry County Rivers Navigability Report: Salem, Oregon, Division of State Lands, 15 p.

Gurnell, A.M., 1997, Channel change on the River Dee meanders, 1946–1992, from the analysis of air photographs: Regulated Rivers—Research and Management, v. 13, p. 13–26.

Hughes, M.L., McDowell, P.F., and Marcus, W.A., 2006, Accuracy assessment of georectified aerial photographs—Implications for measuring lateral channel movement in GIS: Geomorphology, v. 74, p. 1–16.

Komar, P.D., 1997, The Pacific Northwest coast—Living with the shores of Oregon and

Washington: Durham, North Carolina, Duke University Press, p 195.

Kondolf, G.M., 1994, Geomorphic and environmental effects of instream gravel mining: Landscape and Urban Planning, v. 28, no. 2-3, p. 225–243.

Kondolf, G.M., Lisle, T.E., and Wolman, G.M., 2003, Bed sediment measurement, *in* Kondolf, G.M., and Piegay, H., eds., Tools in fluvial geomorphology: Chichester, John Wiley and Sons, p. 347–395.

Maguire, Mike, 2001, Hunter Creek watershed assessment: Gold Beach, Oregon, Prepared for the Hunter Creek Watershed Council, 122 p.

Mount, Nicholas, and Louis, John, 2005, Estimation and propagation of error in the measurement of river channel movement from aerial imagery: Earth Surface Processes and Landforms, v. 30, no. 5, p. 635–643.

O'Connor, J.E., Wallick, J.R., Sobieszczyk, Steve, Cannon, Charles, and Anderson, S.W., 2009, Preliminary assessment of vertical stability and gravel transport along the Umpqua River, Oregon: U.S. Geological Survey Open-File Report 2009–1010, 40 p.

Oregon Department of Transportation (ODOT), 2010, Bridge inspection reports, Pontis Version 1.1.1, accessed 11/2010.

Peck, Hilaire, and Park, Chris, 2006, Hydrology report, *in* Grigsby, K., Coastal healthy forest treatments, Environmental assessment, Analysis file, Chetco, Gold Beach and Powers Ranger Districts, Rogue River–Siskiyou National Forest: 75 p.

Pratt, D.J., 2004, Gravel removal operations and fish habitat planning, Curry County, Oregon: Gold Beach, Oregon, Curry County Department of Public Services, 114 p.

Ramp, L., Schlicker, H.G., and Gray, J.J., 1977, Geology, mineral resources, and rock material of Curry County, Oregon: State of Oregon, Department of Geology and Mineral Industries Bulletin 93, 79 p., 2 pls.

Wallick, J.R., Anderson, S.W., Cannon, Charles, and O'Connor, J.E., 2010, Channel change and bed-material transport in the lower Chetco River, Oregon: U.S. Geological Survey Scientific Investigations Report 2010–5065, 68 p.

Wallick, J.R., O'Connor, J.E., Anderson, Scott, Keith, Mackenzie, Cannon, Charles, and Risley, J.C., 2011, Channel change and bed-material transport in the Umpqua River basin, Oregon: U.S. Geological Survey Open-File Report 2010–1314, 133 p.

Walter, Cara, and Tullos, D.D., 2009, Downstream channel changes after a small dam removal—Using aerial photos and measurement error for context; Calapooia River, Oregon: River Research and Applications, v. 26, no. 10, p. 1220–1245.

Wilcock, P.R., Pitlick, John, and Cui, Y.T., 2009, Sediment transport primer—Estimating bed-material transport in gravel-bed rivers: Fort Collins, Colorado, USDA Forest Service, Rocky Mountain Research Station, General Technical Report RMRS–GTR–226, 78 p.